THE INEVITABLE

GREAT AMERICAN RESET

RIDING THE ECONOMIC ROLLERCOASTER OF CAPITALISM

CARL W HAFELE CFA CPA

ISBN: 1493742175
ISBN 13: 9781493742172
Library of Congress Control Number: 2013920769
CreateSpace Independent Publishing Platform
North Charleston, South Carolina

PREFACE

As a maturing teenager in the 1970s, I naturally questioned why my Grandfather Irwin was someone I had never met. I became even more concerned and curious as to why Uncle Leo—a steadfast, stoic, yet humorous Catholic priest—very frequently was a guest at our house as my pseudo-Grandpa. Uncle Herb, also a priest, was a frequent guest, too.

My wonderful father, Will, gently explained to me that his father "went down with the Crash." What he was actually intimating to me was that Grandfather Irwin *really* went down in the Wall Street Crash of 1929, and after that fateful Black Tuesday, his life unraveled. He was a leveraged car dealer who went belly-up, leaving his uneducated wife and mother of six children—including my Pops—to flounder in a life of destitution and hardship. My father was destined to live the life of a bum, but by the grace of God he was raised by Leo, Herb, and the Church.

My inquisitive nature led me to explore the details of an era, particularly the quality of life (or lack thereof) that my father experienced during the Depression. The harsh reality of what he and his family experienced was very interesting to me. My fascination with economics and its effect on the everyday lives of people was born.

After studying hard to earn three advanced degrees and working three decades in the money management business (including nearly a decade as a university "real world" professor)—all throughout some remarkably fluctuating economic times—I remain the eternal optimist. However, many of us seem to be incognizant of the unfathomable repercussions sure to follow in the wake of the abysmal economic period we currently live in. The future will force us into an undesirable state of flux—and hastily—if we don't open our eyes to this collective reality and make adjustments very soon.

The Inevitable GREAT AMERICAN RESET: Riding the Economic Rollercoaster of Capitalism presents my analysis of our situation while informing and educating you on the growing urgency that we change—while we still can! My hope is that this book entertains and inspires you to become a part of any organization that promotes change.

Financial crises are simply a part of capitalism. The 2007 version was anything but a normal crisis, and its fallout will be evident for years to come. If we focus on the importance of sound economic policies as Priority #1, we will recover. We'll take a look under the hood of the USA economic machine and explain what all this could mean to your investments in the future.

I opine vehemently on the perils of ignoring current trends. I also have included an entire section on the history of financial crises, for to understand the future, we must study the past.

The concepts herein are presented in an easy-to-understand format, meant to assist you in grasping how important it is to "right the ship" now, and how you may lend a hand to the righting. Most of all, as my Mother Shirley always said, "Enjoy yourself—it may be later in life than you think!"

ABOUT THE AUTHOR

CARL W. HAFELE, CFA, CPA

Carl W. Hafele, CFA, CPA is a money manager, professor of economics and finance, and an avid reader of economic history.

Formerly CEO and portfolio manager at National Asset Management and later INVESCO, Carl's experience includes managing over $20 billion in assets. With nearly thirty years investment experience, he teaches investments and other economic courses at Bellarmine University and has taught internationally. Currently, Carl is a Managing Director and Principal at Lanier Asset Management and a Financial Consultant at First Kentucky Trust Company. He remains an active investor in the equity, venture capital, private equity, and real estate markets.

Mr. Hafele is a Chartered Financial Analyst (CFA) and a Certified Public Accountant (CPA) who received his Masters of Business Administration (MBA) in Finance from Xavier University.

Carl is an avid all-around sports fan, and has coached basketball and soccer for many years. A private pilot, Carl is active in numerous philanthropic organizations and a member of the CFA Institute. He and his wife Marianne enjoy travelling, exercising, and "having a blast" with their seven children.

TABLE OF CONTENTS

PART I. THE FINANCIAL CRISIS OF 2007-2009

The Financial Crisis of 2007-2009 (hereafter a.k.a. the Financial Crisis and at times simply the "Crisis") led to the Great Recession, which stands in line as the second worst economic period in modern American history, behind only the Great Depression. This crisis had all of the negative portions wrapped up into one—defaults, foreclosures, bankruptcies, and bailouts. Let's look at some of the events and policies leading up to the crisis and then the events of the crisis themselves. A view of the long hangover and slow recovery seems appropriate, and then let's theorize about the causes, who's to blame, and some key observations. Part I of this book focuses solely on the Financial Crisis of 2007-2009 and ponders whether this crisis is truly over—an excellent question before we analyze key economic policy options and our post-crisis decisions.

Virtually every American was bruised badly by the Crisis, whether they know it or not. Without question, this was the largest economic event of my lifetime. The negative wealth effect from a stock market crash, augmented with the real estate crash, directly affected most

Americans, and the resulting economic contraction affected the rest. Who's to blame? The answer is not that simple. The carnage was so extensive that we've been left with more than enough blame to go around to the many contributing parties.

CHAPTER 1
THE REALITY OF THE GREAT RECESSION

What we know about the financial crisis is that we don't know much.

~ Paul Samuelson
Famous Economist

It was a dark and gloomy night, in so many ways... October 20, 2008. At 2:15 a.m., my beautiful wife, Marianne, came down the stairs in our gorgeous home to find me sitting at my desk, staring into space.

"Are you okay, honey?" she gingerly inquired, her voice quivering at the ghost white expression on my face.

"I don't really know, honey," I muttered. "The world is officially in a 1929-like economic meltdown, and I think we have lost over 50% of our investments and net worth—at best!" Tears flowed down both my cheeks.

My wife, stoic and steadfast, hugged me and lovingly whispered, "We will be okay, Mr. H." There was nothing but silence during the longest hug of my lifetime.

What we now know as The Great Recession was in full swing, and my early morning trepidation was prompted by the events of the past few weeks, highlighted by a scene seemingly out of a horror movie. Federal Reserve Chairman Ben Bernanke, appearing before Congress in an attempt to explain what actually was happening to our financial system, looked as terrified as any human being I have ever laid eyes on. The whites of his eyes were virtually red, as if he'd had a long night with both Mr. Jack Daniels and Maker's Mark. A "deer in the headlights" snapshot on steroids. Our financial system had cracked, and we could hear the sickening thuds of its crumbling foundation.

Perhaps a tad more persnickety with my finances than your typical entrepreneur, I was at my desk that early morning to theoretically "mark to market" the value of all my assets. I also theorized what the values would be when the carnage was over. Municipal bonds would be marked down 50% as defaults would appear everywhere à la the housing default tsunami, which was in full destruction mode. While stocks were already down over 40% from their 2007 highs, they would drop another 20%—levels quickly closing in on ones similar to the 1929 crash. Real estate ventures would totally wreck the balance sheet, compliments of leverage. Private equity would fetch perhaps 25 cents on the dollar due to severely reduced asset values; the illiquidity of such ventures (and their associated bank debt) would likely not be renewable. All in all, thirty years of 70-hour work weeks—*poof!*—up in smoke, virtually overnight.

Even though several of us "saw it coming," there simply was not enough time or conviction to totally avoid the storm. Sure, one can lighten up on exposure to the equity markets, which I had done a year earlier with the assistance of our technical indicators. The other "risk assets" categories including venture capital, private equity, and real estate are quite different when it comes time to sell—because it's practically impossible!

What on God's green earth had happened? Was it a singular event like the September 11th Al-Qaeda attacks or the December 7th, 1941 bombing of Pearl Harbor that changed the world over? Unfortunately, the answer is just not that simple.

CHAPTER 2
THE BUILDUP: 1999 TO 2007

It took us years to get into the mess we got ourselves in at the end of 2008, and it's going to take a while to get out. We lost eight million jobs, we saw a financial system near collapse, and we have a continuing housing crisis that we're making progress on dealing with.

~ Robert Gibbs
Sr. Campaign Adviser to Barack Obama

A series of economic policies and trends occurred during the eight years prior to the Great Recession including:

A. Lowering of Credit Standards (a.k.a. "Houses for Everyone Syndrome")

B. Extremely Low Interest Rates (a.k.a. "The Greenspan Put")

C. High Household Debt Levels (a.k.a. "Load Up The Debt Truck")

D. Investment Bank Leverage Levels (a.k.a. "Lever Me Up, Too!")

A. HOUSES FOR EVERYONE SYNDROME

To find the origins of the crisis, one must go back over a decade to the work of Congress and the change in lending standards. In the mid-1990s, banks were forced by the Department of Housing and Development (HUD) to extend a higher percentage of their loans to below-median income households.

I would like to summarize and simplify this change as a formidable decline in the underwriting standards for residential housing. First, the requirement was that 40% of loans granted had to be issued to below median-income households in 1996. This was raised to 50% in 2000 and raised yet again to 56% in 2008. I fondly refer to this phenomenon in my classes as "Houses for Everyone Syndrome." The Clinton Administration really turned up the heat in 1999, and even the *New York Times* forewarned that a bailout—à la the savings and loan debacle in the 1980s—may occur in an economic downturn. Being an owner of Fannie Mae and Freddie Mac stock personally and for my clients since the early 1980s, we quickly exited—which was, as it turns out, an excellent investment decision. It was based on my belief that you just don't mess with the "invisible hands" of the economy too long, because if you do, something is bound to tilt the scales in the wrong direction!

Lower down payments and more debt relative to one's income became commonplace. More leverage equals more risk. You kind of got the feeling this was going to end in a not-so-cool fashion.

From the banks' perspective, granting credit became much less emotional and far more calculating (pardon the pun). Lend the money by granting a mortgage, take a nice fee, and promptly sell it off in the secondary market to Fannie Mae or Freddie Mac, the government-sponsored-entities (GSEs) created by Congress. Yes, we all assumed they were backed by the government. The share of mortgages being held by the GSEs increased significantly in the 1990s, and peaked at approximately 45% in 2002. Yes, our Congress was messing with the "invisible hands" of free markets, and the outcome from government intervention shouldn't be surprising, yet always is. The politics and lobbying that occurred around the hugely profitable relationship between the corporate officers of the GSEs and the politicians receiving donations fueled the fire. A credit bubble was in the making.

If you haven't heard enough about the not-so-free lunch market antics of Congress, review the Community Reinvestment Act (CRA). It modified standards in favor of minorities and low-income applicants. Most had little to zero down payments and less than stellar credit histories. And history showed that such mortgages had a default rate multiple times (estimates vary but some say as high as ten times) the typical "prime" loans held by middle and higher income American homeowners.

Financial engineers created securitization of these mortgages, which is nothing more than bundling them up into standard debt securities called mortgage-backed securities. Investors can then own the mortgages, and a large market evolves. Everyone wins—the mortgage holder, the bundler, and the investor.

Both the growing role of Fannie and Freddie, as well as the quality of the loans, are noteworthy when discussing the roots of this financial crisis and its buildup.

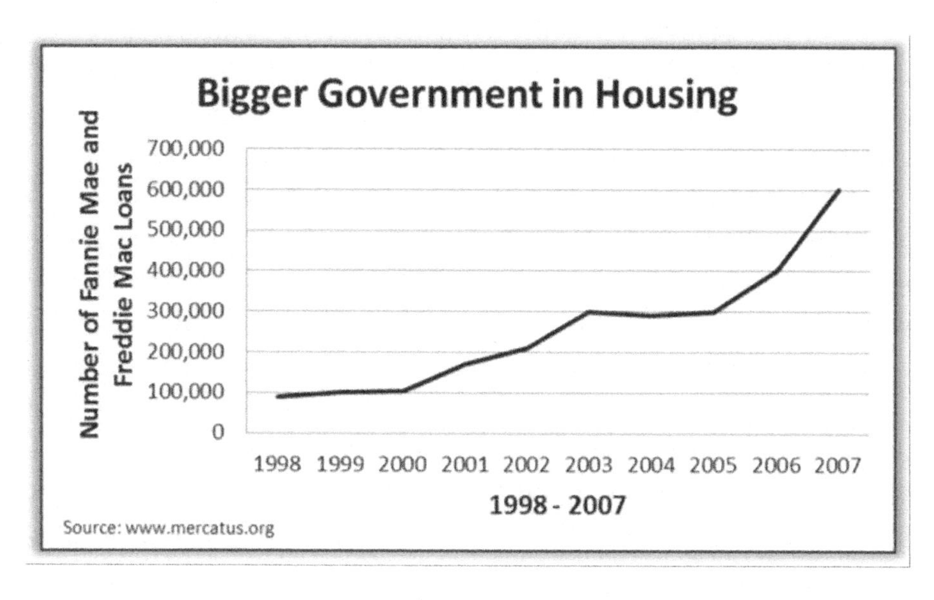

The number of loans extended by Fannie and Freddie skyrocketed from less than 100,000 in 1998 to over 600,000 in 2007. And the quality of the loans deteriorated, as more people put fewer dollars down when purchasing a home.

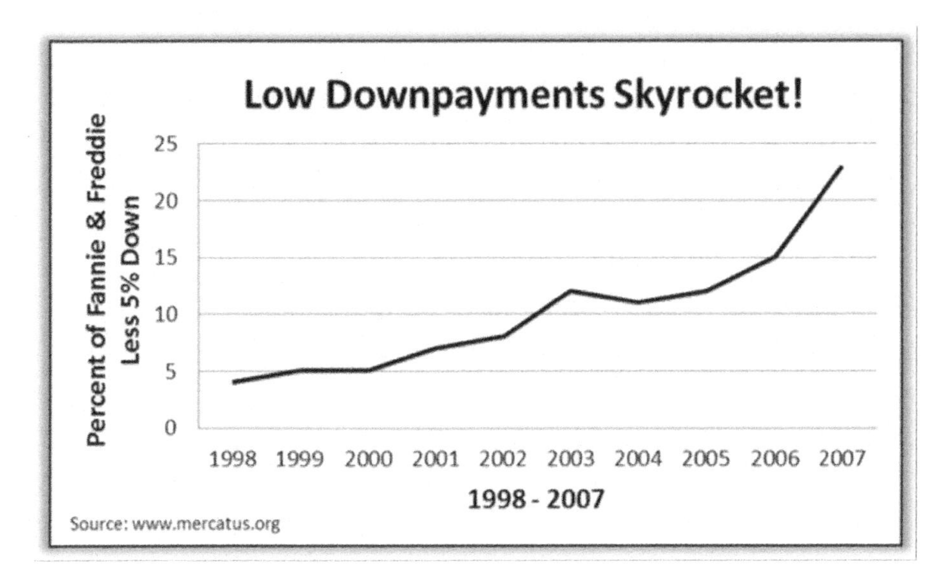

The percentage of loans with less than 5% down rose from less than 5% in 1998 to nearly 25% in 2007. My father would describe that as having "no skin in the game." I grew up with the rule that you saved 20% of the purchase price before buying the starter home, as well as the spouse's dream home.

A basic principle in capitalism is that most thriving businesses in the free market are guided by a leader that has time, talent, and treasure invested. If you have your own money at risk, odds skyrocket that you will be successful. But having 95% or more on credit definitely qualifies as having no skin in the game. Human nature would predict defaults.

Thus, the moniker of "Subprime Financial Crisis" is often applied to this gargantuan Financial Crisis of 2007-2009. Subprime loans have very low down payments and large mortgage amounts relative to one's income. Their cousins are "Alt A Loans," loans made without verification of income or even the existence of a job. The regulations were also loosely applied by lenders regarding higher credit applicants. An overall reduction in lending standards occurred. What an excellent example of financial innovation/liberalization, as well as mismanagement of this new revolutionary concept! Some severe side effects were sure to manifest.

One phenomenon my research and experience has still not figured out is how the leaders pulled all this off for so long. Fannie's CEOs Franklin Raines and James Johnson received huge bonuses for many years in their respective tenures, and the demise of the entire housing market left taxpayers holding the bag. Both Fannie and Freddie were declared insolvent in 2008 and taken over by the U.S. Treasury. Granted, the leaders had a tough dilemma—fulfilling their fiduciary duty to shareholders while playing the political game that included large donations to the Congressmen supporting the scam. Unbelievably, CEO Raines and CFO Tim Howard were tried for their roles, exonerated, and live comfortably on their $340 million and $20 million golden parachutes. In the words of John Mellencamp, "Ain't that America, you and me!" We paid for that!

Later, Ben Bernanke would succinctly describe all the increases in mortgage defaults simply as a function of a decline in underwriting standards. And the housing boom was bubbling—if we could only just get some real low interest rates…

B. THE GREENSPAN PUT

The primary goal of the Fed should be price stability—keeping inflation very low (like in the 2% to 4% area). If they can successfully avoid higher inflation, as experienced in the 1970s, and avoid deflation (negative inflation) à la Japan in the last twenty years, the other economic variables usually perform—in theory—quite well. GDP will advance nicely and unemployment should stay low. Of course, fiscal policy must be sound, and indeed it was through the Reagan, Bushes, and Clinton eras.

Alan Greenspan, the "Maestro," assumed the Fed Chairman position in 1987 at the request of Ronald Reagan. Following in the footsteps of the successful inflation hawk Paul Volcker, Greenspan quickly gained credibility in the October 19, 1987 stock market crash by promptly providing liquidity to a shocked America. His eclectic style and monetarist view contributed greatly to a very palatable economic environment, led by his slow, predictable interest rate moves from 1987 through 2000. He was in the middle of establishing himself as the greatest Fed Chair of my lifetime—perhaps ever—having led U.S. monetary policy through our best economic times since the Roaring Twenties. And then what my father always lectured me about happened to the "Maestro"—he got a "big head."

As the dot-com bubble burst in 2000 and the stock market commenced its 30% decline, the U.S. entered its first recession in ten years during 2001. On September 11, 2001, the towers of the World Trade Center were destroyed and the war on terrorism further shocked the economy. More deterioration occurred when the accounting scandals of Enron, WorldCom, Arthur Andersen, and more were revealed.

From 2000 through 2002, amidst all sorts of turmoil from a number of sources, Greenspan lowered the Fed funds rate from over 6% to an unheard of and unfathomably low rate below 2%.

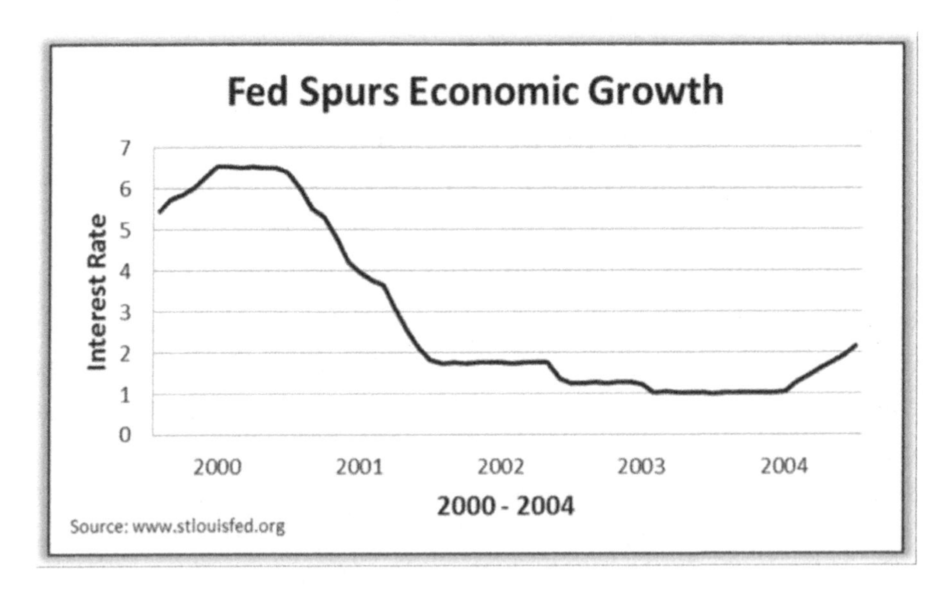

The Fed funds rate determines all interest rates and is followed as a summary of monetary policy in normal times. Most all interest rates are altered when the Fed funds rate is changed.

One can see the Fed funds rate was quite normal before plummeting in 2002 to 2% and remaining there for two years.

This easy accommodative monetary policy became known by many as a "Greenspan Put." The put refers to a put option, which allows one to sell an asset at a predetermined price to another party (the put buyer) if the price declines below the predetermined price. In effect, this is downside protection, or a type of insurance. Fed to the rescue!

The 2002-2004 *put* was one of several of the Greenspan era. Others included his reactions to the 1987 stock crash and September 11 attacks—successful short-term tactics to prevent economic recessions after a shock to the system. But this one associated with the bursting of the Internet bubble lasted over two years.

With regulation changes from Congress in the mortgage market in place for a few years, a Beverly Hills Supper Club fire was percolating (I actually assisted in the haunting experience of pulling out some of the 165 bodies from the rubble of that 1977 tragedy in Southgate, Kentucky). With super low interest rates, relaxed lending standards, and aggressive marketing by homebuilders and bankers, the panacea was growing.

C. LOAD UP THE DEBT TRUCK!

And let's make the already-low interest rates available to you super low by making your mortgage adjustable! So let's buy a huge mansion! Adjustable-rate-mortgages (ARMs) are pegged to a short-term interest rate like the Fed funds rate, and payments are altered periodically as interest rates change. So let's say the Fed funds rate was 2%. Virtually anyone could get a 4-5% mortgage if not lower, and have a down payment of just 3%. Some loans were called "2/28" loans—guaranteed super low teaser rates for two years and then a more normal rate for the remaining 28 years.

ARMs have been around for decades, and in 1990 they represented less than 10% of all mortgages. I've never had one, as I have always valued home payment predictability. My theory states that you simply refinance if rates go lower, and importantly, never participate when interest rates go up. But with bankers pushing the super low rates, which meant very low payments, ARMs increased to over 20% of the loans in the U.S.

It is important to note that ARMs had only slightly higher default rates than the more traditional fixed loans through 2004. This should not surprise us, as we had not experienced a period of substantial interest rate increases since inflation was tamed in the early 1980s. There were very few ARMs in those volatile years.

So no matter what our nationality or marital status or risk-taking posture may be, just back up the truck and shovel in the debt!

Below is a 50-plus year history of household debt as percent of disposable income—the best measure of how much debt the average household owns.

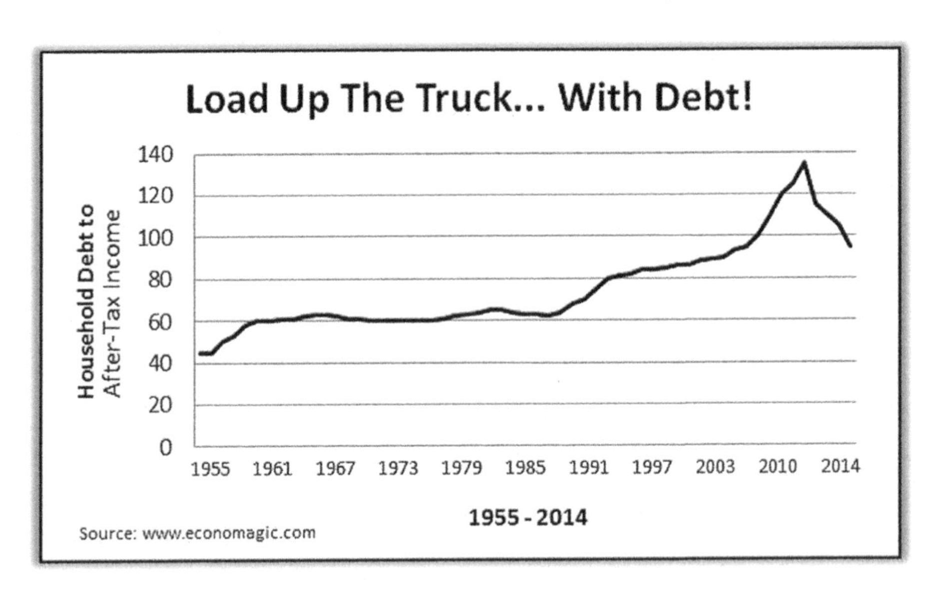

For the first half of my lifetime, households typically took on debt as a percentage of after-tax income to the tune of approximately 60%. Then the ascent began in the early 1980s as a function of ever-lowering interest rates, the growth of Fannie and Freddie, and simply an increase in overall certainty in the economy. Tax rates were drastically lowered and economic activity was extremely solid—let the good times roll! This ascent took debt levels to approximately 90% by the late 1990s while economic super-progress not only continued but accelerated. The last five years of the century were wonderful times as the Internet went to Main Street and the wealth effect of the stock market propelled many into a lifestyle beyond their wildest dreams.

Yet another ascent commenced, and the sharp rise in debt went to unprecedented levels, peaking in 2007 around 135%. This level is skyscraper high—more than a doubling of the 60% rate consistent with the 1960s, 1970s, and early 1980s. A 25-plus year period of the "leveraging up" of America!

With large debt levels on homes and a large amount of loans being adjustable, an increase in interest rates would ignite a rolling-over of home prices that would have devastated the economy. And that's exactly what happened, commencing in mid-2006, and continuing through 2008. Homeowners could not afford to pay the higher payments and many that could pay simply did not as they were "upside down"—a term previously used for many auto loans. If the fair market value of the asset is less than the balance on the loan, the asset is classified as "upside down."

D. LEVER ME UP, TOO!

Investment banks are basically underwriters of securities and do not take deposits like regular banks. The Securities and Exchange Commission (SEC) changed the regulations in 2004 to allow the investment banks to issue more investment holdings relative to its capital base, thus leveraging up just like the households did—but on steroids! For mortgages with a AAA rating, leverage was allowed at an incredible 60 to 1 ratio. Investment banks expanded their mortgage departments with a focus on buying loans with literally pennies on the dollar and packaging them up in a process deemed securitization. These banks then obtained excellent credit ratings on these bundles from the rating agencies, who received nice fees for the ratings. Investors believed it all—until the default rates increased and the house of cards was revealed.

Is there any reason why anyone would attempt to stop the party? Investment banks and rating agencies were being rewarded handsomely. Ethics? What does this have to do with ethics? As my father always warned, "People will do anything for two things: power and money."

Classic factors seen in other financial crises that we saw here in the buildup were financial innovation, a difficulty in valuing assets, an increase in uncertainty, a housing bubble forming, and agency problems with investment banks, loan providers, and rating agencies.

THE EUPHORIA OF THE BUILDUP

I talked much with my family about the lunacy of unqualified borrowers (by my standards) owning homes, the incredibly low interest rates, the high-level of debt my friends were taking on, and the leverage on Wall Street. In one of my discussions, when my daughter asked how I felt about the looming crisis, I replied, "Sad and sick."

Yet I will never forget one of the happiest events I experienced right before the Financial Crisis of 2007-2009. My next-door neighbor at my winter home in Scottsdale, Arizona was a very nice lady approaching her mid-forties. Let's call her Penelope to protect the innocent. Penelope purchased the home for the then-fair market value of approximately $700,000 in 2003. She was a computer technician, and I estimated from our casual conversations that she earned approximately $70,000 a year. I wondered how she could afford a home valued at ten times her income. Yes, Penelope was fully levered—she had borrowed $665,000, which meant her down payment was a whopping 5%.

Fast-forward three years to January 2006. It was not uncommon to receive unsolicited offers on your home in that crazy time, and Penelope got one for over $1 million. In amazement, she asked me what she should do, as she never had any savings in her life. So Penelope had the opportunity to put $250,000 into her bank account after tax, which I advised her to accept… and she did indeed sell. Whether due to luck or a prophecy of what was lurking around the corner, Penelope now had a balance sheet! And the best part of the story is that she saved it all, except for a small portion which was spent on her breast augmentation. I had never seen such a huge grin on her face—whether due to her savings account or her breast augmentation.

Penelope's story provides an opportunity to illustrate an example of ROI—return on investment—in which the investor enjoyed an incredibly positive aspect of leverage. A net profit of $250,000 on a $35,000 investment over just three years is seven times (plus!) your money, or nearly an eye-popping 100% gain per year. When it rains, it pours! Penelope was so blessed NOT to be on the other side of the mountain in housing prices that peaked in 2006, like so many unfortunate Americans were.

By the way, in all my infinite wisdom (sum: zero), I did not take my *own* unsolicited offers, selling later just above my 2003 purchase price (bye-bye, swimming pool and its hassles). Can you say round trip? I later purchased a condo in foreclosure at 40% of the 2006 price (hello, zero maintenance). That, folks, is what I call riding the economic rollercoaster of capitalism!

CHAPTER 3
THE BUST: 2007-2009

Housing was Ground Zero for the Great Recession. Between early 2006 and the Obama inauguration in 2009, average house prices fell by a third across the country. In certain areas... house prices fell by more than half.

~ Mark Zandi
Co-founder & Economist, Moody's Analytics

In 2004, then Fed governor Ben Bernanke proudly stated that the U.S. economy had transformed into a period of low macroeconomic volatility that was dubbed "The Great Moderation." Good times were had by all with few and shallow recessions. In addition, the inflation dragon remained caged.

All of the policy changes we made had favorable outcomes (or so it seemed), and any side effects were not yet visible. More people were buying nice homes with low down payments and low monthly payments. The packaging machines were rolling, the goods were all stamped "high quality," and there were plenty of buyers of the securities. A beautiful concoction!

With the cocktail already mixed, inflationary fears started to bubble in mid-2004—quite a natural reaction due to the lag effect of monetary policy as well as two-plus years of Fed funds rate at 2%. Chairman Greenspan began a series of slow, methodical one-quarter or one-half of 1% interest rate increases, bringing the important rate back up to

5%+ by mid-2006. As the ARMs reset, the large subprime market began seeing an increase in the number of defaults. Housing prices "rolled over" and the downward spiral began. In addition, the levered financial system participated, realizing huge losses on their previously thought-of AAA rated securities. An implosion!

The housing bubble burst—and man did home values plummet!

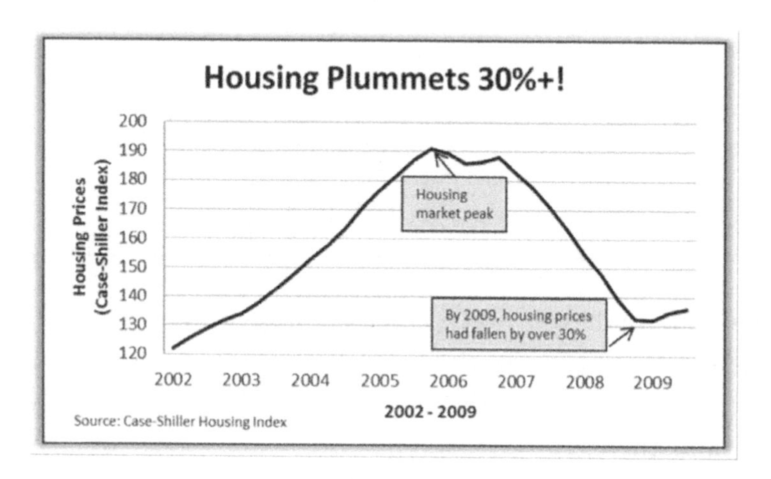

The most often used indicator of the housing market is the Case Shiller Housing Index. It shows that housing prices declined over 30% in 2007-2009, erasing virtually all the buildup from the 2002-2006 four-year increase. It was a steady three-year retreat.

Investors throughout the world began to feel the effects. First, the hedge funds that held the lower-rated "tranches" of mortgage securities lost their shirts, and the higher-rated securities were undressed. It was not pretty. As these securities were held worldwide, an international impact occurred and a complete loss of trust in the financial marketplace ensued.

As the crisis accelerated in the latter part of 2007, the Fed reversed course.

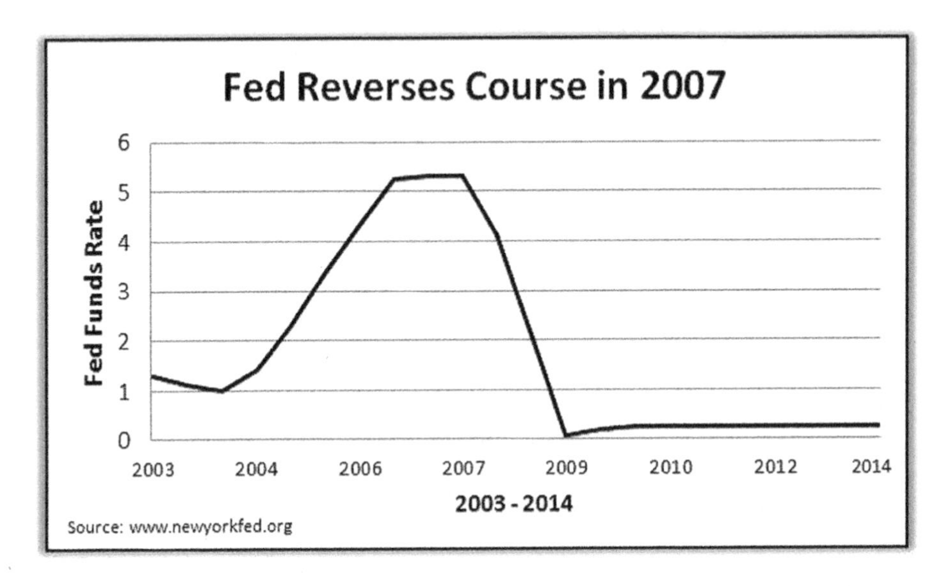

The Fed funds rate was decreased in a faster fashion than its ascent, signifying a realization of the serious nature of the crisis at hand. The rate fell to nearly zero in approximately two years—and still remains there!

The Fed also provided an unprecedented amount of liquidity to the system in October 2008. It promptly pumped up the size of its balance sheet to over $2.2 trillion from approximately $800 billion, nearly tripling the money supply. There were numerous Fed programs from October 2008 that were phased out the subsequent year but replaced with buying mortgage-backed securities. The government programs included opening up emergency lending facilities for banks to guarantee subprime mortgages. The stock market—the best leading economic indicator—continued to decline.

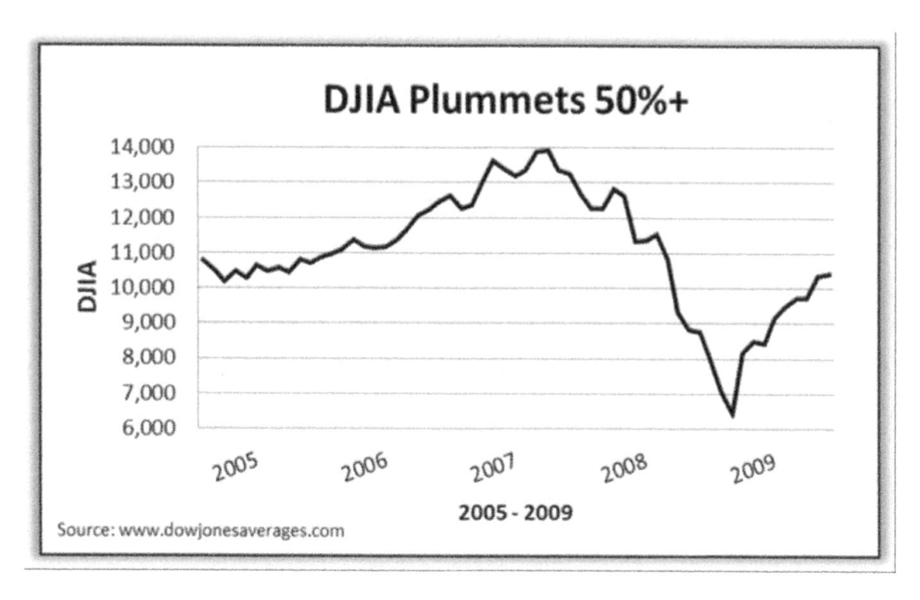

The market peaked in October 2007 and the downfall continued into early 2009, bottoming on March 9th, 2009 at 6,440… down over 50%.

The failure of high profile public firms was another predictable part of the Financial Crisis, and the landscape was scattered with victims. Bear Stearns was forced to sell itself for pennies on the dollar to J.P. Morgan. National City was forced to marry PNC shortly thereafter. Lehman Brothers went bankrupt. Merrill Lynch was purchased by (of all people) Bank of America—a cultural oxymoron if I've ever seen one. Wachovia was taken over by Wells Fargo, a function of Wachovia's Countrywide Credit acquisition and its huge portfolio of ARMs. Washington Mutual sold to J.P. Morgan. AIG was bailed out. These are some of the biggest names in the history of the financial markets!

Much of the above occurred in just two months—September and October of 2008. In addition, the Reserve Primary Fund "breaks the buck"—a phenomenon where the money market mutual fund value of $1 was no longer the value. The TARP (Troubled Asset Relief Plan) was introduced and provided a $700 billion bailout package. The government bought subprime mortgage assets from financial institutions or simply injected capital into them. GM and Chrysler were bailed out and later went through bankruptcy in mid-2009.

Without question, by late 2008, the recession had deepened. Unemployment climbed to 7.4%. More government intervention occurred with the TALF (Term Asset-Backed Securities Lending Facility) which provided liquidity to a frozen and constrained credit market. Mortgages would be "renegotiated" with payment decreases to go down to less than 38% of income –a once revered common-sense percentage but extremely conservative for the boom years.

When our 44th president of the United States was sworn into office in January 2009, President Obama was greeted by a $787 billion government spending program which was then signed and passed. Many, including this author, questioned the wisdom of this Keynesian idealism, as it had been proven ineffective decades earlier. Yes, it was a bold plan in the attempt to avert Great Depression II.

In early 2009, the markets furthered their declines. Housing declines continued. The stock market reversed course when the Administration announced it was going to focus on oversight—perhaps a relief that another futile Keynesian stimulus spending act (rumored $1 trillion plus) would not come to fruition. (Thank the Lord it didn't). Finally, in late March, things started turning the corner a tad, as credit markets started functioning. By summer of 2009, economic contraction was minimal and the unemployment rate that had increased to 9.5% reversed course.

But the unemployment situation was murky throughout 2009. The duration people remained unemployed grew longer—extended benefits for the unemployed without question was and remains a major influence. Benefits were extended to 99 weeks (approximately 23 months) from the traditional 6 to 9 months, illustrating the widespread nature and severity of the financial crisis.

By the end of 2009, Americans felt, quite simply, bruised. With net worths still significantly less compared to frothy 2006 levels, consumer confidence was way below the typical range. Lower home prices and lower savings—typically the two largest sources of one's net worth—were the contributors.

However, the global financial system's descent into what seemed like an eternal spiral turned around and a depression was averted. Which policies worked, which policies made it worse, and which were in between is a huge controversy… and probably will forever remain so. I liken this debate to the impact of the FDR New Deal Programs on the recovery from the Great Depression. Did they help or did something else (like time and/or war) help? Or did the New Deal policies only prolong the pain? Nobody knows, nor ever will!

With huge deficits and a very large Fed balance sheet in today's market, time will tell. The Financial Crisis of 2007-2009 was a hulking, 800-pound gorilla. Regarding the wisdom behind a large and growing amount of regulation in an attempt to avert another financial crisis, time will also tell.

CHAPTER 4
THE HANGOVER... AND SLOW RECOVERY

In these times of the Great Recession, we shouldn't be trying to shift the benefits of wealth behind the curtain. We should be celebrating and encouraging people to make as much money as they can. Profits equal tax money. While some people might find it distasteful to pay taxes, I don't. I find it patriotic.

~ Mark Cuban
American Businessman & Philanthropist

The hangover from the build-up and the bust is a pretty brutal one, and our recovery from the Financial Crisis remains a very slow and mild one. In this chapter, we will discuss why.

Normally, when a recession occurs, the recovery snaps back like a rubber band, driven by the business cycle. The most frequent comparison made to the 2010 recovery is the recovery associated with back-to-back recessions in 1980 and 1982—a period now frequently labeled as the third worst economic period. Having lived through it, I have some vivid memories and recall a period of many questions and experiments in economic policies.

The current recovery, put simply, has not been very strong despite unprecedented monetary policy accommodation. The answer to why the recovery has been slow and mild lies with the economic players called business people. Our evaluation of sound, fiscal policy (or lack thereof) presents pause. We have experienced a leveraging-up phenomenon for decades and the opposite—deleveraging—is a definite reality. We must thus deal with the facts! As demographics drive entitlements up, spending has been continually increasing. As deficits grow from the spending, the debt piles even higher. As the debt goes higher, the typical reaction is for tax rates to increase. And as higher tax rates discourage investing, fewer jobs are created and less tax revenues are generated. Those who dispute these facts—that business minds think this way—are not business people.

I kindly challenge any person or entity to convince me otherwise. With the tax rate increases in 2013 plus the additional Affordable Care Act (a.k.a. "Obamacare") tax, those of us who are educated, work hard, and pay taxes at the higher marginal rates now pay 25% more in taxes than we did in 2012! The marginal taxes are on any additional income—whether it comes from a consulting gig or working overtime! Going from 35% federal rates to 44% accounts for that 25% increase. It's sad to say, but we haven't seen anything yet! Have a cold one and play a round of golf! Forty-four percent is the federal tax alone! Add on the others and it's a heaping 70% marginal tax rate... which means I get to keep 30%. I may not be that smart but I know I will *not* bust my butt to keep 30 cents of every dollar I make. Other things are more important, such as exercising, coaching, and other "enjoy life" moments. After-tax ROI is a concept politicians can't grasp as they spend recklessly and continue to ask the businessperson to pay for it!

Another reason the hangover has endured is the ongoing super fight with asset deflation. This may be the largest repercussion of the Financial Crisis. And the Fed has been valiantly fighting deflation by its ultra-accommodative monetary policy since October 2008. Fast forward to 2014, the FED's asset buying program was tapered by $10 billion each FED meeting. Thus the stimulative buying was scheduled to be complete by yearend, finally taking the pedal off the medal! The unintended consequences, which I am certain will be seen in coming years, will materialize. The size of the experiment is simply unprecedented!

Deflation simply means that prices will be cheaper next month, so why would you buy anything today? GDP growth slows. Look at Japan's growth for the last few decades. In the U.S., we have not experienced deflation since the 1930s, where asset values decreased in nominal terms. The piece of property becomes worth less than it was a few years ago and/or what you paid for it. From the 1940s through 2006, there were periods where asset values went down in real terms, but inflation kept them from going down in nominal terms! You just don't *feel* as bad if you can sell it for what you paid for it and break-even—even though after inflation, you probably lost money. But selling it for less—thank you, Great Recession—really hurts!

And the wealth effect is also an influence on the slow recovery. When your house is worth less, and your savings are not what they once were, most people are hesitant to open their wallets. *Honey, you know that summer trip to the Cape or the Hamptons we've been discussing? Let's resume our conversation next year.*

In summary, the private sector's unhappy view of unsound fiscal policy, the significant tax increase of 2013, the potential for continuing rising tax rates, a fierce fight battling deflation, and the negative wealth effect combine to explain the slow-recovery experience. A punishing and lingering hangover indeed...

CHAPTER 5
THE BLAME GAME

Blaming speculators as a response to financial crises goes back at least to the Greeks.
It almost always is the wrong response.

~ Laurence Summers
Economist & Harvard Professor

Many are to blame for the Financial Crisis! Much finger-pointing has been leveled at one or two groups—shame on these people as they are either politically promoting their plight, side-stepping appropriate blame, or are simply not well informed! I'll present to you the seven groups that should share the blame and my reasoning for each.

(1) GOVERNMENT OFFICIALS

The first and largest source of the problems is that we seem to have ignored the history of Keynesianism and the fact that it does not work! The regulation favoring "Houses for Everyone" was simply awful. The actions of HUD and CRA backfired. Specifically, you cannot outsmart Mother Nature without creating a storm. We forced it, then pushed it to the brink, and eventually went over it. Government is not stronger than the natural forces of the free market. If it tries to be, bad stuff happens—politely called "unintended consequences."

(2) POLITICIANS

The political back-scratching by the heads of Fannie and Freddie and the politicians was criminal. Had they ever asked the question I always ask in any ethical dilemma, "How would that look on the front page of the *Wall Street Journal*?" much of the criminal action would not have materialized. The heads were asked to serve two masters: the shareholders and Congress. Saying no to Congressmen is analogous to telling your father to go away after he has given you money.

(3) SECURITIES and EXCHANGE COMMISSION

The SEC relaxed the leverage laws in 2004, allowing the investment banks to lever up at ridiculous levels. It really aided in the termination of the "Great Moderation" and the associated permanent taming of the business cycle. Such leverage could work—but only when trees grow to the sky.

(4) THE FEDERAL RESERVE

Chairman Greenspan was appropriately concerned with the recession of 2001, the terrorist attacks of September 11, 2001, and the stock market crash of 2000-2002. He reduced the Fed funds rate to 2%, a very radical move at the time. Economic growth was his focus as opposed to the primary mandate of price stability and low unemployment. Simply stated, the "Maestro" just got too cute! The stock market crash of over 30% was totally appropriate. Valuations were 30 times earnings driven by the Internet froth. Let the free markets work freely! There was no need for super-low interest rates.

(5) THE RATING AGENCIES

The AAA stamping of mortgage-backed securities by Standard & Poor's and Moody's was also criminal. I will never believe that the models used did not show what would eventually materialize regarding defaults and foreclosures. Instead, they kept pushing on with a wink, collecting huge bonuses until the party blew up.

In their defense, I must state this was indeed all new territory with lowered standards, originate-to-distribute lenders, ARMs, 2% Fed funds rate, low down payments, no skin in the game, high debt as percent of income, and other variables. Not to mention that home prices had never materially gone down in history. However, nobody was concerned that any of these items may not work forever, and that the associated buildup may possibly end. Our educational institutions on capitalism and the business cycle are not getting the job done. I say this in the framework of studying history as well as from an ethical perspective. I teach as I was taught—that leverage is a dual-edged sword!

(6) WALL STREET

Financial engineering and innovation is an excellent part of capitalism! But the packaging of mortgages and getting them stamped AAA by their buddies at the rating agencies was immoral and deceitful. There is no way that securitizing loans into diversified pools means a AAA rating is appropriate. Bonus city baby! I wish some of those bonus dollars would get paid back to the bailout funds. In addition, the investment bank leverage levels left no room for any errors.

(7) MAIN STREET

It has been said that as housing goes, so goes a nation. We all love to see Main Street do well! But the problem we ran into was just trying too hard to help them, and our regulators and innovators just got Main Street over-levered and in very big trouble!

Every man and woman in America should be responsible for themselves, health permitting. If you are told that you can legally jump off the bridge and not get hurt, should you do it? If you can live in a $600,000 house on a $75,000 salary with a $35,000 down payment that took you five to ten years to save, should you do it? You can only say yes to the first question if you are a real thrill seeker. Regarding the latter question, the answer is only yes if you *know* that a new period (à la 2002-2006) including suspiciously low interest rates and an upcoming sizzling hot real estate market is just around the corner.

IN SUMMARY...

Plenty of blame can be spread to plenty of groups!

Congress appointed a six-member committee named the Financial Crisis Inquiry Commission to ferret out the causes of the Financial Crisis. In early 2011, the committee released the findings in a report. On the same day in January, three members of that committee issued their own summary in a memorable *Wall Street Journal* article, giving a dissenting view of the committee's findings. In addition, one of the other commissioners dissented and presented yet another viewpoint.

Say what? Six members published findings and four members dissented? That sounds like conflicting viewpoints, eh? The only logical explanation is partisan rhetoric. And that is exactly what Americans are livid about, including this still-enraged old codger.

The official findings of the report solely blamed Wall Street and its influence on Washington. Wall Street manipulated the system, making huge personal gains. This was unquestionably the left side of the political spectrum. These findings supported drastic reforms to the financial system. The Dodd-Frank Wall Street Reform and Protection Act—the most comprehensive act of all time that alters our entire financial system—with its 848 pages, was indeed just and justified, per this school of thought.

The one dissenting commissioner blamed government intervention with Fannie and Freddie for causing the housing bubble that triggered the crisis. This viewpoint represented the conservative right.

But the other three dissenters presented an educated and truly bipartisan viewpoint in the *Wall Street Journal* article. They professed that the causes of the Financial Crisis were a complex set of ten factors worth mentioning. These included (1) a credit bubble, (2) a housing bubble, (3) non-traditional mortgages, (4) toxic financial assets (securitization), (5) concentrated risks in housing, (6) too little capital (leverage), and (7) super low interest rates. In a synergistic way, the combination of the above variables caused (8) a contagion—a ripple effect—which resulted in (9) a shock to the system, whereupon high profile firms failed. Finally, this led to *panic!*, and thus (10) a severe economic contraction.

I concur with all three authors of the *WSJ* article, particularly that it is very dangerous to oversimplify a crisis of this magnitude. Promoting a policy that is politically-driven will not help end the crisis. And, by golly, it could just make it much worse!

Why is this important to note? It illustrates why we must educate ourselves and ignore much of the partisan rhetoric that we hear today. Nobody wants to step up and admit any guilt, and thus the recovery time is protracted. Sad, but it's just human nature.

In spreading around the blame for the Financial Crisis of 2007-2009, I have appropriately ignored one very important concept. Regarding the policy responses associated with the recovery, government officials are pro-Keynesianism, pro-government, pro-regulation, pro-taxes and, oh my, pro-spending. Combined, these ideologies would definitely thwart economic growth rates in every era in every country. Many contend that the long hangover after the Crisis is a function of these policies.

Most importantly, what have we learned from the buildup, the bust, the hangover and slow recovery, and the futile process of pointing angry fingers of blame associated with the Financial Crisis of 2007-2009?

First, the only sure way for all of this to happen is by the high usage level of debt. We need sound policies to limit leverage for prosperity.

Second, messing with the invisible hands of capitalism and free markets is always more complicated than one originally thinks, particularly when experimenting with new concepts and tools. There always seems to be some secondary unintended and unpleasant side effects.

Third, regulation always has someone's good intentions in mind, but economically it can sometimes be absurd. Regulation almost always has some bad unintended consequences associated with it. We need a common sense approach to regulation that instills confidence yet appropriately penalizes the non-conformists.

And last, we need leadership. Our country has been through the ringer and is experiencing a long hangover that will still take years to overcome. Policies to help lessen the blow—ones that make the recovery time shorter and the next recession shallower—are essential.

PART II. THE IMPORTANCE OF ECONOMIC POLICIES

We have discussed our huge financial crisis now known as The Great Recession. There was a large amount of buildup in the years preceding the bust in 2007 to 2009, and the hangover and slow recovery are not surprising given the magnitude of the recession. Many are to blame.

In this section, we'll discuss why economic growth is so important for the quality of our lives. Fiscal and monetary policies are very influential to economic growth, and we'll assess the current status of both. We'll also visit the folly of Keynesian economic policies, and look at two countries—Japan and Canada—for lessons on what works and what simply does not work.

CHAPTER 6
QUALITY OF LIFE AND THE IMPORTANCE OF ECONOMIC GROWTH

The business of America is business.

~ Calvin Coolidge
30th U.S. President (1923-1929)

Business is like riding a bicycle—either you keep moving or you fall down.

~ Anonymous

What do we mean by making the economy grow? Why do we care if we grow at 1% per year versus 3% per year? What are the effects of inflation?

First, GDP is defined as the market value of final goods and services produced within the country during the year. It is the best measure of economic activity used by all countries. It is most often calculated by summing up consumption, investment, government spending, and net exports.

We measure economic growth by using GDP and subtracting inflation; we call this "real GDP."

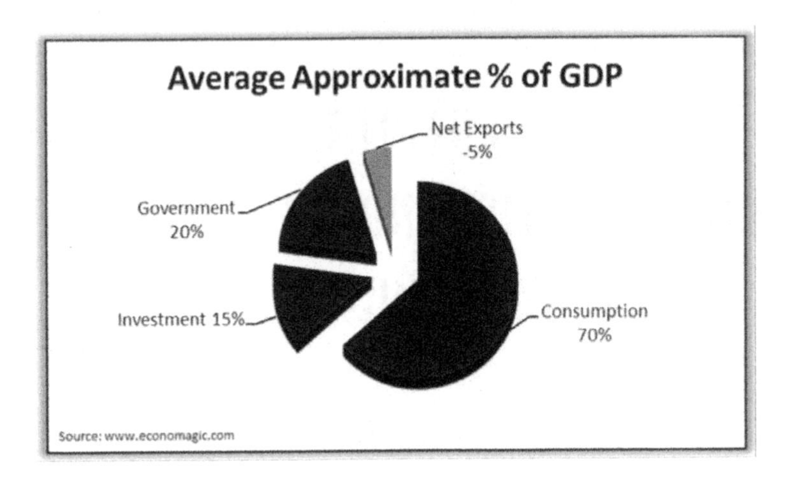

Note that consumption—you and me buying everyday items like food, gasoline, and toiletries—represents the lion's share of our economy. We must feel good and confident about our everyday economy for it to smoothly progress. Investments in plants and equipment—items that promote job growth—are also important. Government spending normally is about 20% of our economy, and net exports are negative 5%, which means we are importing more than we are exporting.

What has been the history of economic growth? A 3% growth rate after inflation is our historic norm and our forward-looking goal.

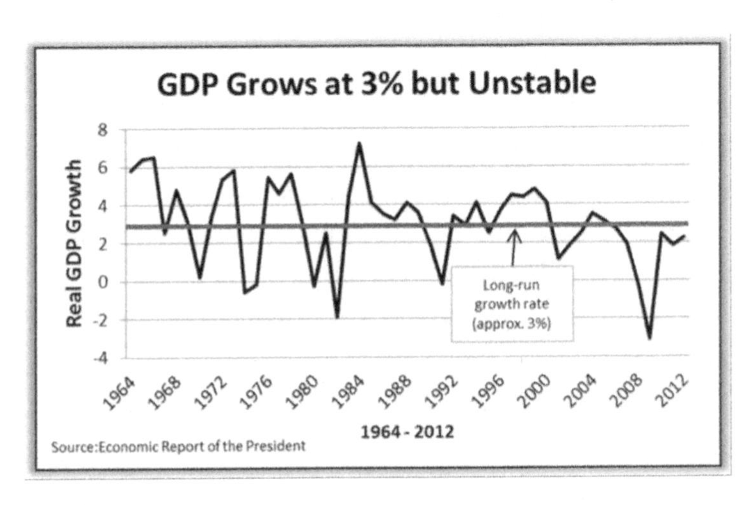

Since 1960, the real GDP growth rate has been 3% with much less volatility in the 25 years from the early 1980s to mid-2000s. During periods of recession, GDP growth typically crosses below the zero line.

GDP growth rate is the best measure of the quality of our lives. Sure, it has its drawbacks, but it is an excellent barometer and there exists no effective alternative.

So why is growth so important? I have long believed the answer is best summarized using the "Rule of 70." Simple math shows the magic of compounding using this rule.

$$\frac{70}{\%\ \text{increase}} = \text{Doubling Period}$$

Using an annual real GDP growth rate of 3% gives us a 23-year doubling period—which means life gets twice as good in a short 23-year period if you grow at 3% after inflation.

Has that formula and growth rate worked in my lifetime? Absolutely yes!

My skeptical students are silenced when I ask if there would be anything wrong with making this statement thirty years ago: "I called my brother on my cell phone, while making a reservation on my computer, while using WiFi to fly Southwest—all while watching a cable show on my big screen."

Sorry ladies and gents—there were no cell phones, home computers, WiFi, Southwest Airlines, cable TV, Internet, or flat screens. Solid GDP growth rates are essential and have produced all of these technological advancements and wonderful improvements in the quality of our lives.

Investor confidence produces capital investment, which results in greater productivity—a key to real GDP growth and a higher standard of living.

The truest measure of the quality of life is to view the progress of GDP on a per person basis.

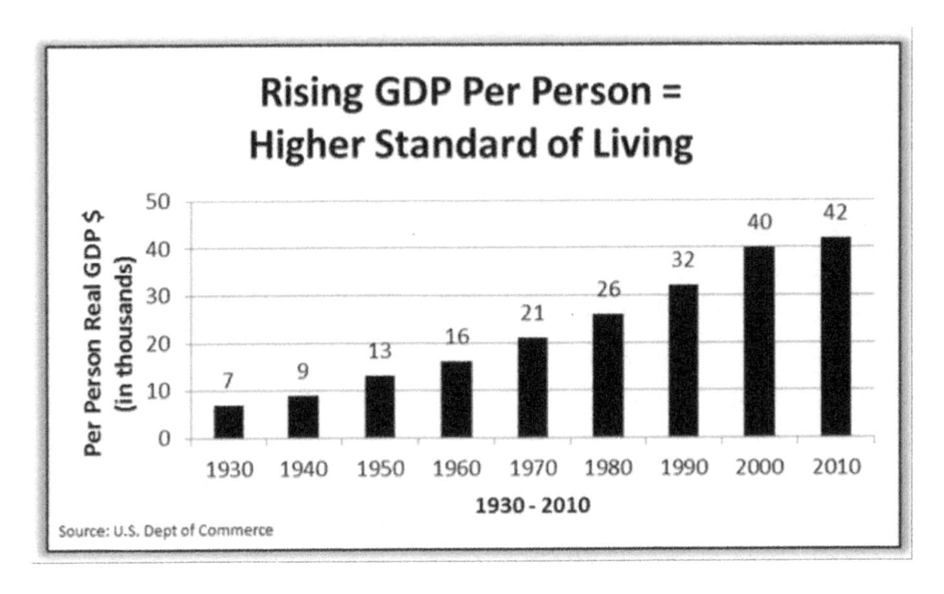

Per capita GDP is simply GDP for the period divided by the population, with all figures first being inflation-adjusted (here to 2005 dollars). This allows a true apples-to-apples comparison.

In 1940, when my father, Will (now 90), was a teenager, per capita GDP was $9,000. Fast-forward to 1980, when I was exiting my teenage years, it had nearly tripled to $26,000. My life literally was nearly three times better than Will's, particularly when you hear him tell his life stories.

By 2010, GDP per capita grew to $42,000—a phenomenal six-fold increase in the quality of life in approximately the span of one's lifetime of 80 years. But if we had just a 1% growth rate, the quality of life would have slightly more than doubled, using the Rule of 70. A huge difference in lifestyles!

One drawback of GDP is that it does not measure the "underground economy," which includes unreported income and illegal activities. Experts estimate it is about 10% of the total economy in the United States, and a much higher percentage in more socialistic European countries.

So if economic growth is so important, how do we get it? Economists collectively agree that in normal times, we can obtain additional growth from increasing demand and/or increasing supply. Increasing demand occurs when three things happen: growth in our personal balance sheets (called the "wealth effect"), increased optimism about the economy and our lives, or a decrease in interest rates. Increasing supply also occurs when three things happen: an increase in resources (such as the Beverly Hillbillies finding oil "out back"), technological advances such as the Internet, or new institutional policies that bolster productivity.

As the subsequent chapters will illustrate, most of the policies implemented today do not address any of the above six ways to promote economic growth. If a policy doesn't fit one of the methods to increase supply or demand, it will not assist in the advancement of GDP. It will in fact decrease the quality of our lives.

The importance of solid economic growth is clear. And it is derived from sound economic policies. So fasten your seatbelts and let's look at the key economic policies and tools of measurements that have molded GDP growth.

CHAPTER 7
FISCAL POLICY: RESPONSIBILITIES AND CURRENT STATUS

We in Scotland need fiscal responsibility.
Quite simply, we need to be responsible for what we raise in taxes and what we spend in taxes.

~ Tom Hunter
Scottish Businessman & Philanthropist

There are two government bodies that direct economic policies—one for fiscal policy and one for monetary policy. Here we discuss fiscal policy, with monetary policy being the topic of the next chapter.

Fiscal policy is simply the responsibility of our federal government, led by the trio of our President, House, and Senate. From an economic viewpoint, the government has four responsibilities:

MANDATE	A.K.A.	COMMENTS
1. Grow GDP	Economic growth.	3% absolves many sins.
2. Maintain Price Stability	Inflation 1-3%.	Avoid high 1970s-like inflation; avoid deflation (a la Japan).
3. Maintain Full Employment	Natural unemployment rate of 5-6%.	Safety net size influences behavior.
4. Deficits & Debt Responsibilities	"Fiscal Responsibilities"	Debt grows if deficits are higher than 3%.

To execute these mandates responsibly, our elected politicians have just two means of doing so: (1) taking revenue out of the economy in the form of tax revenue, and (2) deciding how much of that revenue should be spent, including which government programs are funded. Simplistically speaking, the government's role is to tax and spend.

Let's expand on each of these key mandates.

GROW GDP

We have presented the history of GDP growth since 1960 and the 3% desired rate. But it is noteworthy that our growth rate over the last ten years has slowed significantly to approximately 1.5% annually. This is definitely a problem because the Congressional Budget Office (CBO) assumes a 3% growth rate in their projections.

MAINTAIN PRICE STABILITY

This is more the responsibility of the Fed than the President. It is important to note that the U.S. needs to have a 1-3% inflation range for solid economic growth with limited volatility. Below 2%, we risk deflation (a negative inflation where prices go down), à la Japan. Above 4%, à la the U.S. in the 1970s, measures become distorted and resource allocation (in an attempt to figure out what effects inflation will have next) thwarts economic growth. Inflation has not been an issue for several decades now due to a proper focus on the avoidance of deflation.

MAINTAIN FULL EMPLOYMENT

Policymakers focus on maintaining an unemployment rate at a "natural rate" of approximately 5%, with small, cyclical fluctuations associated with the business cycle. The "natural rate" is a function of two types of unemployment. Structural unemployment is a more permanent type, defined as a fundamental mismatch of skills or location between an employer and potential employee. Frictional unemployment is a function of time searching for work or a transition between jobs.

Unemployment insurance—an "automatic stabilizer" along with progressive tax rates— helps to smooth out the cyclical fluctuations by paying benefits for a period of time to laid off workers.

We remain above the "natural rate" as we recover from the Great Recession. This is not surprising based on uncertainty surrounding the huge deficits, rising tax rates, and extended benefit periods for unemployment compensation. Unemployment has been slowly going down in recent years, but remains above the natural structural level of approximately 5%.

DEFICITS and DEBT RESPONSIBILITIES

This is a very large economic variable, and is the major problem child of recent times since 2007. In attempting to grow GDP at a 3% rate, while maintaining a low 1-3% inflation rate, and having unemployment at its natural rate, the policymakers' responsibility of keeping the annual deficits and cumulative debts has not been upheld. Facts are facts—regardless of your religious, political, or socioeconomic preference.

The best way economists measure fiscal responsibility is the annual deficit/surplus as percent of GDP. The annual deficit or surplus is simply the difference between the revenue brought in from taxes and the expenses taken out by spending. We'll look further at these levels and driving forces, but the arithmetic below sums it up for each year since 1950. For us accounting and finance types, this is simply the bottom line of the income statement for the individual calendar years.

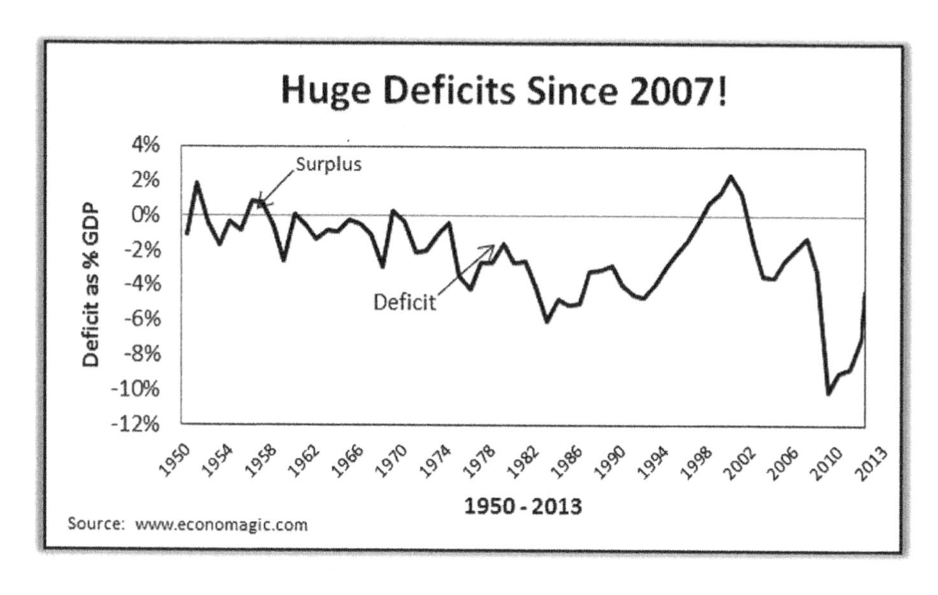

Some key observations:

1. Deficits are common at the 2-3% range for many years without much harm. The vast majority of economists concur that 2-3% deficit levels are OK—as long as GDP is growing at that rate or higher. Assuming so, the cumulative debt as percent of GDP—the best measure of how much we owe relative to the size of our revenue—does not increase.

2. Until recently, our record postwar deficit was a whopping 6% in 1983, as we experimented with Reaganomics and took tax rates significantly lower to spur investment—a phenomenon that indeed materialized in subsequent years. Thank you, Art Laffer, for educating us about the importance of incentives! President Reagan listened, and off to the Roaring 80s and 90s we went. Oh what a memory!

3. A glimpse at this chart reveals the four surplus Clinton years in 1997-2001 as a beautiful memory in life. The Internet boom

drove the stock market boom, as revenues were 20% of GDP and spending was held steadfastly around 18%. Solid economic growth produces huge amounts of tax revenue! And this is done without tax rate raises! We don't need a war to get growth. We need incentives!

4. But finally, and sad to note, observe our deficits since 2008. They are unprecedented—except in 1941 when we spent beaucoup dollars to extinguish Hitler and save capitalism. The CBO projects more large deficits for many years to come! Stay tuned for more on the source of the deficits—spending—which is driven by the growth of entitlement programs, propelled mainly by the aging of America. We are in lock step in our march to socialism.

Equally as important as the deficits is the summing up of them to quantify our total debt. For the accountant types, this summarizes all the prior years and is known as the balance sheet. For others, it simply answers the question of, "How well, financially, is the business doing?"

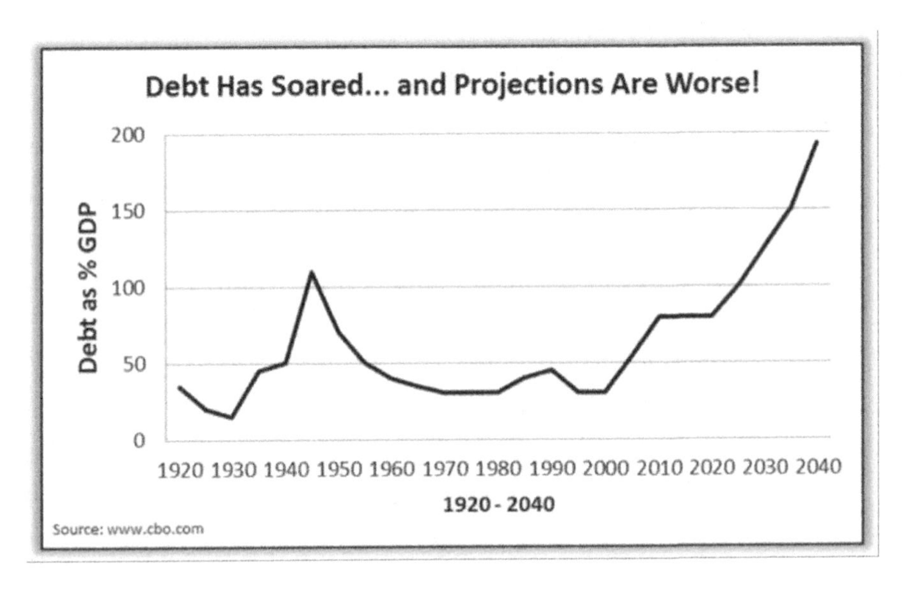

As with the prior chart on deficits, debt is also best analyzed as percent of GDP. For over 200 years of our great nation's history, with the 1940s defense of capitalism being the exception, we maintained our debt levels at a manageable 25-45% of GDP. So let's center on 35%.

In the four-year period of 2008-2012, the debt doubled to over 70% of GDP.

So my daughter asked, "Am I correct? Am I getting this? We kept debt at a respectable level for over 200 years of around 35%, and in just four years, we doubled it? Is that really possible?" While proud of my daughter's acuity, my response was a melancholy, "Yes, my dear. This thing is a mess, and is heading in the wrong direction."

The budget history and projections are solely functions of spending more than collecting—lower revenue because of low economic growth rates and much higher spending—"like a drunken sailor." We have a monumental spending addiction!

CHAPTER 8
MONETARY POLICY: RESPONSIBILITIES AND CURRENT STATUS

Monetary policy itself cannot sensibly be directed at reducing imbalances.

~ Timothy Geithner
U.S. Secretary of the Treasury (2009-2013)

The second government body is the Federal Reserve which controls monetary policy, defined simply as the management of the money supply and interest rates. The Federal Reserve System was formed in 1913 as a stabilizer to the banking system and an important part of capitalism. The leader of the U.S. Fed is arguably the most powerful person in the world.

A completely different animal than fiscal policy, with (thankfully) fewer political problems and much more potency in its policies, monetary policy mandates are similar to but categorically different than fiscal policies:

MANDATE	A.K.A.	COMMENTS
1. Maintain Price Stability	Inflation 1-3%.	Primary mandate.
2. Maintain High Employment	Natural unemployment rate of 5-6%.	"Other" primary mandate.
3. Assist in GDP Growth	"Monetary Stimulus"	Problem source in 2002-2004 era.
4. Financial Markets Stability	Interest rates and foreign exchange.	Reason for Fed creation in 1913.

Compared with fiscal policy, please note that the responsibility of a balanced budget is absent. The Fed has none.

As I was taught in the 1970s—and personally experienced in the 1980s and 1990s—monetary policy is much more important than fiscal policy. Perhaps ten times more important and potent, a sound monetary policy equates to a flourishing economy. Keep working, establish a nice methodology to saving your hard-earned dollars, keep your allocation to stocks high, and voila! Just thank the Fed chairman for assisting in the establishment of a nice personal balance sheet.

But there's one caveat! The big bear in the room of monetary policy can only be so big, powerful, and potent if its sister—fiscal policy—does not behave very well. That is exactly what is happening, as fiscal policy has been running amok with large budget deficits as percent of GDP. We have experienced the Great Recession, which helped create some unfathomable deficits. Demographics are further digging a huge debt hole through the unchecked growth of the unfunded liabilities of Social Security and Medicare associated with aging baby boomers. This issue is solvable only with major policy changes. Our fiscal policymakers are addicted to spending, and that certainly does not help.

The Fed's toolbox traditionally has contained three items, with the fourth officially added in 2008:

TOOL	DESCRIPTION	STATUS/COMMENTS
1. Reserve Requirements	Sets bank reserves.	Rarely changed.
2. Open Market Operations	Executes policy.	Most often used tool.
3. Fed Funds/Discount Rate	Controls loan rates.	Been near zero for 5 years... and counting.
4. Interest Paid on Reserves	Assists in execution.	Influences banks' excess reserves.

The policy of the Fed, in normal times, is best illustrated by the level and direction of interest rates. All interest rates are a function of the Fed-determined federal funds rate. If the Fed wants more economic activity, it will have a policy that is "accommodating" and it will orchestrate interest rates lower. Conversely, if their desires are "restrictive" to slow the economy, their interest rates will rise.

Interest rates have been in a long-term decline for over thirty years.

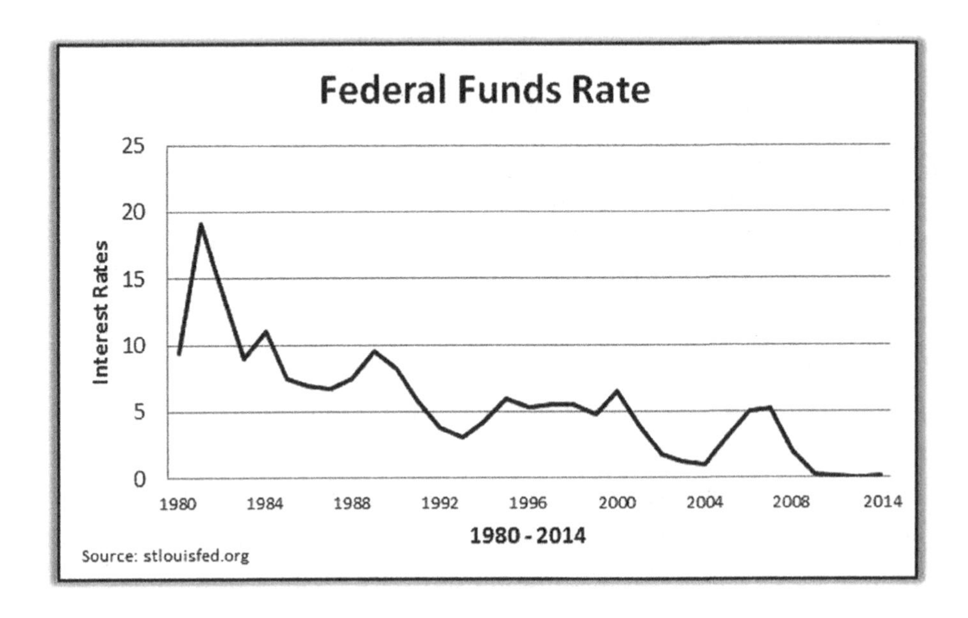

The downward trend in interest rates commenced in 1981, as Fed Chairman Volcker squeezed out inflationary expectations. By the early 1990s, the Fed funds rate stayed pretty close to 5%. Not until 2002, in an attempt to exit the recession associated with the stock market correction and September 11th terrorist attacks, did interest rates go so low. They were methodically raised from 2004 through 2006, then plummeted to zero when the Great Recession commenced. It is important to note they remain there today. This 30-plus year trend of declining interest rates has no more room to go down. You can't have negative interest rates!

Fed policy in light of the Great Recession has been extremely accommodative. As interest rates remained low and economic growth continued to sputter, the Fed commenced an aggressive program through its open market operations, buying bonds to flood the system with money. Yes, it's the equivalent of running the old $100 bill printing press or dropping money out of the helicopter.

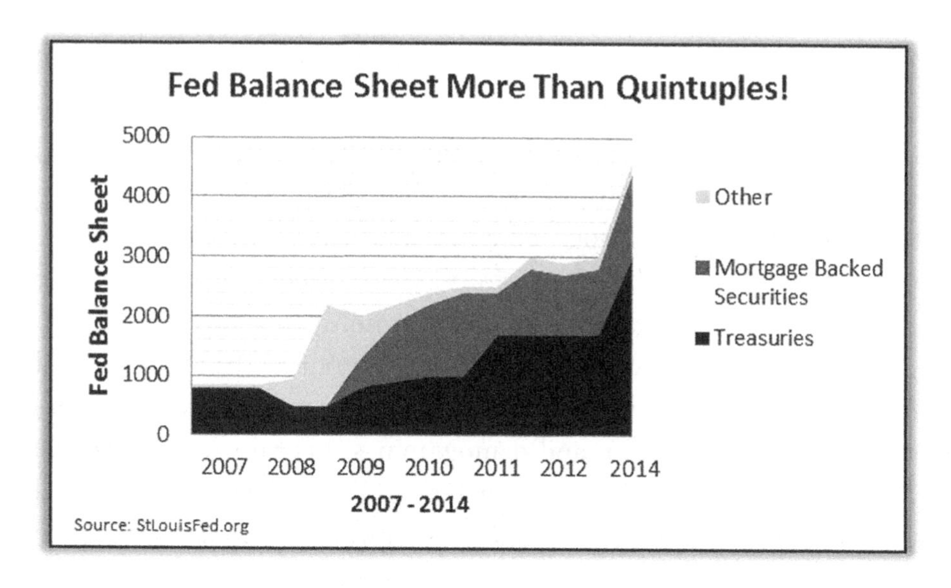

The size of the balance sheet of the Fed is analogous to the amount of money in the system. For years, the money supply was approximately $800 billion, growing at a slow, methodical Milton Friedman-recommended pace. Then, in October 2008, the great American monetary policy experiment commenced. Open the floodgates and here comes the money!

This graph is simplified into three assets that the Fed bought to fatten its balance sheet—U.S. Treasuries, mortgage-backed securities, and other miscellaneous purchases. In the past, as it has been for decades, the Fed owned U.S. Treasuries and little else. Pre-Crisis, the assets were worth $800 billion. But in October 2008, rescue programs provided liquidity to the system and spiked the balance sheet up to $2.2 trillion—nearly triple its original value! These programs were replaced with mortgage-backed securities purchases. In 2014, the total size of the balance sheet will top out under $5 trillion—more than five times larger than a mere six years ago! Note that the amount of mortgage-backed securities purchased by the Fed is now larger than the entire Fed's pre-Crisis balance sheet. Fed announcements to slow the growth of the money supply was like easing up on the gas pedal to slow from 200 MPH to 100 MPH in a 65 MPH speed limit zone. Dangerous decisions!

Other tools have been added to the Fed's toolbox since 2008, and they have indeed been used. Bernanke's famous 2002 speech revealed these other tools and policies—both functions of his former status as a Fed governor and as an historian of the Great Depression.

The additional Fed tools and policies have surfaced in the press as Quantitative Easing 1, 2, 3, QE Infinity, and Operation Twist. Other new tools have included extended time commitments, revelation of targets, and more. All in all, Bernanke is pulling out all the stops to avoid deflation! Japan has experienced very slow economic times for decades as a function of deflation and demographics. Bernanke vows that the United States will not experience such pain! He has been openly critical of the Japanese central bank, which very recently started drinking the Bernanke Kool-Aid and has also turned on the printing press.

There is one eerie caveat I would be remiss to neglect when mentioning Bernanke's brilliance and policies in his 2002 speech. After a decade plus of studying financial crises, he profoundly stated that the U.S. is quite different than Japan because of the massive problems of Japanese banks and corporations and the level of debt that constrained Japan's ability to use aggressive fiscal policy. Sound familiar and applicable to the post-2007 situation here in the U.S.?

With such an experiment in macroeconomics occurring, I applaud Bernanke's aggressive monetary stance. Without it, I am afraid the Great Recession would have been the Great Depression II. The road to recovery—one that we are still trudging along, and will be for hopefully just another three to five years—is very rocky. The lag effects of monetary policy that we know occurred after our 1960/70s stop-go approach will make the coming years quite interesting. And they will be magnified by irresponsible fiscal policy.

The real problem associated with the humongous size of the Fed balance sheet is the velocity of which the money turns in the economy, best measured by the money multiplier. To get economic growth, the money has to circulate. For the fifty years prior to the Great Recession, the money multiplier was between 8 and 12 times. It peaked in the mid-1980s at 12 times, and was approximately 8 times in the 1990s and up to 2007. In the financial crisis, it plummeted to 3 times, which is where it remained into 2014. This is the lowest multiplier rate since this measurement commenced in 1913. Those figures are jawbone dropping scary.

Why is the money not moving, turning, circulating or multiplying? First, lenders are hesitant in doing what they do—they are supposed to lend! Borrowers are hesitant to borrow—including myself! And why are we hesitant? Because of uncertainty that is prevalent due to more regulation, higher tax rates, and the educated guess that the rates will go yet even higher as government grows and grows.

One investment I made pre Great Recession had a three-year term of prime minus one (shorthand for term at the prime rate less one percent), which was 2.25%. Upon renewal in 2010, the bank decided to put a 5% floor on the loan and add some handsome fees despite investors' collateral being fifty times the size of the loan. Just at the time virtually every business was struggling to get by as the world had virtually stopped, this increase was devastating to the entire venture. Investors were livid—and appropriately so! Bad feelings will forever linger about the bankers. And a similar bad taste remains in many of the investors regarding new investments. Slow velocity of money results.

I attended an excellent presentation in 2013 by Dr. Michael McCracken of the St. Louis Fed. The executive summary of the state of the Union is that the economy continues to slowly improve—kind of moving in the right direction. The Fed has begun thinking of the pros and cons of various exit strategies, starting to communicate its plans to Wall Street and has said that fiscal issues probably won't (but could) affect the chosen exit strategy.

I give the Fed credit for its positive, confident tone. After all, that is part of the unwritten portion of their job description. Yet the unparalleled high level of confidence should promote some caution! Let's look at some details.

Earlier we covered the role of the Fed and its traditional tools, followed by additional "other" tools, including the ability to pay interest on bank reserves since 2008. As few as ten years ago, I couldn't fathom in my wildest dreams that we would be using anything but the traditional tools. And as you know, we are using all of them—traditional and "otherwise"—in this great monetary experiment. There exists no prototype for baseline analysis to predict the unintended side effects that will undoubtedly arise in the next few years.

The Fed is witnessing tepid GDP growth and slowly improving unemployment rates. They also see the housing market recovering, a too-moderate 1% to 2% inflation rate, and the continuation of the stock market rally. An exit strategy is in formation, and some estimated timeframes or events that trigger their moves have been made public. The Fed tentatively committed to an unemployment threshold of 6% and inflation over 2.5% as some "forward guidance." These are attempts to help us heal and incent businesspeople to invest.

So if Milton Friedman was correct in his most famous quote, "inflation is always and everywhere a monetary phenomenon," and we have more than quintupled the size of the Fed's balance sheet, then won't we get inflationary pressures soon? Historically, in other countries and in the U.S., when large amounts of money are printed, inflation follows a few years later.

There are several different theories about inflation formation, and I have discussed them with numerous of my Fed-watching buddies. They are:

1. The Fed says that we won't get inflation because they have unbounded confidence in their ability. The proverbial "removing of the punch bowl from the party" will occur with perfect timing. Everyone can have a grand old time, but they'll shut down the bar soon enough so you can safely and legally drive home.

2. The Fed will keep the pedal to the metal, or slow down gradually, desiring a higher, perhaps a much higher, level of inflation above its stated target range. The old "it beats deflation" argument.

3. We will have inflation. Unprecedented balance sheet levels, along with untried and only theoretically safe, newer, Fed tools just cannot work in sync without some side effects. Most guess the main side effect will be higher inflation. ...Didn't we get along just fine in the 1980s for years with 3-5% inflation?

One reason the Fed's confidence level is so high despite the size of its programs is the level of excess reserves. These are defined as capital reserves held by banks in excess of what is required by the regulators. They have skyrocketed since the asset purchase plans went wild in 2008.

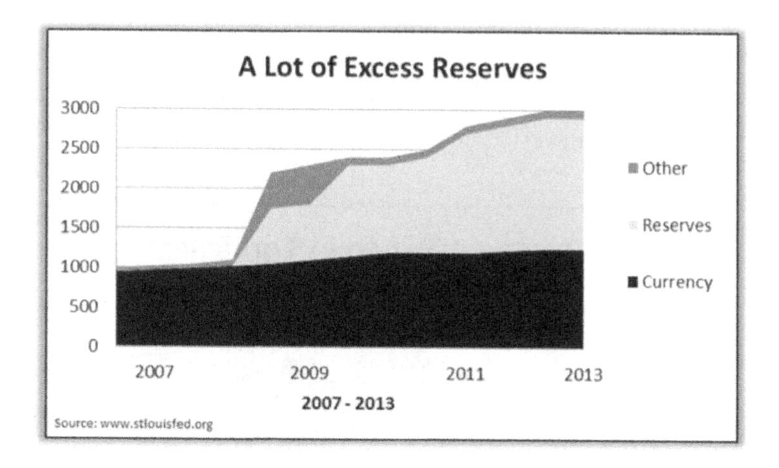

This illustrates how little demand for near-zero interest rate money exists today. The Fed can put the money out there, but the entrepreneurs (like me) don't want any! And those who do want to borrow go to the bruised and bandaged banks who want to lend only to the healthy balance sheets.

The banks still have plenty of problem properties that they never dreamed of foreclosing. Many of my friends have lost large percentages of their net worth—I call it the preview to "The Great American Reset"—if not their entire wardrobe. Many of us may be wondering for a long time, "Just when is it safe to go back in the water?" So thank you, Mr. Banker, but no thanks.

Eventually, we hope, these high levels of excess reserves will be put to work in our economy. The Fed can then mechanically execute its exit strategy. But regarding the amount and timing of unwinding the experiment does not warrant such confidence. Have we ever done anything really well the first time?

The Fed's plans are clear and rather explicit, appropriately always subject to change. Take the foot off the accelerator in 2014 and eventually stop buying. In addition, allow existing mortgage-backed securities to mature, effectively tapping on the brakes. In 2015, they start raising the Fed funds rate followed by selling some treasuries. They may also employ their new interest on reserves tool that Congress authorized in 2008.

The interest on reserves tool can make an impact quickly but not without cost. It could more than double bank profits by paying a rate of say 3% on excess reserves.

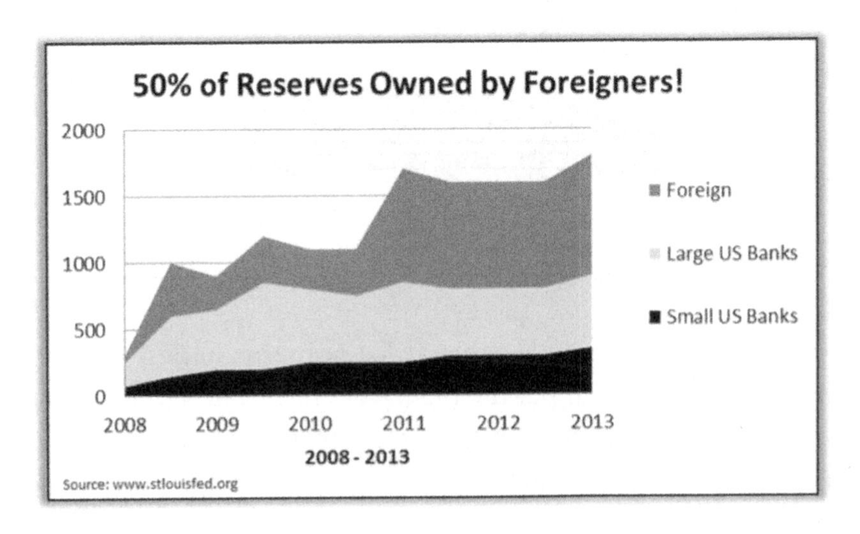

The portion of excess reserves owned by foreign banks is noteworthy. Minuscule pre-Crisis, foreign banks now have approximately 50% of the excess reserves. So, half of any interest payments using the new tool would go to foreign banks. Yikes!

But most alarming to me is the Fed's lackluster view of fiscal policy. I wanted to ask the Fed representative just why they beat their chest so hard and scream so loudly—like some kind of suit-wearing Tarzan. *Aah-yee-aah-YEE-AAHHH!!!* The Fed just openly does not buy into any of the research and common economic worries about debt as percent of GDP. They admit that if we do not put ourselves on a sustainable budget path (so far, zero progress) and people think we are monetizing the debt (yes), then people may find a safer haven than the U.S. (I am starting to investigate now), and we will get higher interest rates and higher inflation. Yet the Fed nonchalantly says we are nowhere close to the "tipping point," simply because we are the USA! It's a "we are just too big and too good looking" mentality. All this is deeply disconcerting to this student of the game!

The dollar is indeed the global reserve currency, so there is a strong demand for dollar-denominated assets. But the Fed proudly puffs that the U.S. has its own powerful monetary authority that can credibly dilute the value of the debt via inflation and credibly act to promote economic growth and thus grow tax revenue. WOW! Can anybody conceive that they are *that* good, or that such action is a plausible remedy? If so, why have we made the mistakes of the last decade? The Fed is on everybody's list of people (except its own) who contributed to the Financial Crisis of 2007-2009. Prolonged low interest rates from 2002 through 2004 were a huge contributor to the housing boom and bust which was at the heart of the Crisis. Oh, such godlike powers and such short memories! It will be very interesting to look back at this whole mess in 2020.

Janet Louise Yellen, Chair of the Board of Governors of the Federal Reserve System, was selected to replace Ben Bernanke in January 2014. Considered an excellent choice by most, she is the first woman to head the

Federal Reserve of the United States. Yellen is considered to be a "dove," meaning she is more focused on lowering unemployment than fearing inflation. But does anybody really think the new Fed Chairperson can pull this off without some miscalculations? The odds of a completely smooth landing in such a storm are low.

Thankfully, the Fed does acknowledge there are some dangers. Executing the strategy too soon could thwart the economic recovery and put the patient (the economy) back into intensive care. Nobody has witnessed a switch from such an accommodative monetary policy before because one has never existed. I'd bet the odds of exiting too soon are less than 10% with the new Chair.

Yet another danger is the reverse scenario: exit too slowly, excess reserves fall, the multiplier increases, and inflation increases dramatically.

The Fed stoically hypothesizes it can remove the punch bowl in a timely manner and the inflation increase will be slow, moderate, and healthy. The "Superman Fed" will guide the "invisible hand" without a hiccup. I hope they are right, but I put the odds at 25%—thus, I wouldn't bet on it.

What is likely to happen is we will get a jolt of inflation followed by a steady rise in inflationary expectations for years. I believe that is exactly what the Fed wants—to pay our huge debt with cheaper money. Monetizing the debt is intentional, although not professed to be so. Why not? Most Americans don't understand this concept and it would undoubtedly be a political hot potato. The spending binge in Washington will cause us to simply pay more for things with money that is worth less. Policymakers' memories have faded concerning how difficult it is to get out of the inflationary spiraling-up syndrome, and avoid the accompanying inflationary expectations. Everyone who has saved will have plenty of money—it just won't buy much!

CHAPTER 9
SO WHAT'S NEXT?

The nine most terrifying words in the English language are, "I'm from the government and I'm here to help."

~ Ronald Reagan
40th U.S. President (1981-1989)

Both monetary and fiscal policymakers have taken unprecedented measures to avoid a 1930s-style prolonged period of debt deflation. The Fed's balance sheet has quadrupled and Washington has spent more dollars than any period in history (except the 1940s to defeat Hitler).

Will we be successful in avoiding the big bang moment where the economy really derails? If so, which policies worked? How do we know? Are there other countries who have tried these remedies? Did they work? Proponents say our activities have kept us out of the Great Depression II and the associated 25% unemployment (about 15% if calculated as we do today), 25% plus drop in GDP, and 25% deflation. Pundits point to the debt doubling and the 100% "tipping point" research of Professors Rogoff and Reinhart, which we'll later discuss.

Well, we do indeed have some history and some answers. But, overall, we are officially in unchartered waters. Without question, it is an experiment. On a scale from 1-10, yes it's a 10. A real experiment!

I will bet my antique automobile play-toy (it's a 1972 Oldsmobile 442) that there will be some unintended consequences from our fiscal stimulus and monetary experiment. History suggests a lot of not-so-palatable events may occur—including defaulting on the debt, a currency crisis, or a serious, prolonged bout with inflation.

The return to the already-refuted Keynesian style of fiscal policy—prime the pump 'til she gets running—is ludicrous. Policymakers' only justification to return to the outdated theory is based on the Great Depression, when we did too little, too late, or did the wrong things. Our knowledge of monetary policy was at a third-grade level. Keynes-speak prefers to spend a lot quickly when a recession is at hand.

I'd bet you anything that John Maynard Keynes would turn over in his grave over the lack of fiscal prudence when we were in good times! When economic growth is strong, you should bank a little bit of those tax revenues, not spend them. What ever happened to the notion of "saving for a rainy day?" The savings fund got politically shelved in the back of the bottom drawer. Keynesian philosophy, ill-fated as it has been, stresses two parts: spending in bad times and saving in good. The latter never rose from the dead, but the spending sure jumped up quickly. A re-realization that Keynesian economics does not work must materialize.

Debt levels at home, in Washington, and across the globe have all risen substantially in my lifetime. So what's next?

The Great Depression in the 1930s and several other pre-1900 depressions all lasted a long time—usually eight to ten years. That would suggest our hangover should be gone in approximately three more years, around 2017. Or are we kicking the can down the road for an even larger Great Recession II, or something called "The Great American Reset"?

Debt levels will soon be huge and unmanageable if the trends continue. A conservative estimate would be $20 trillion and the all-important number—debt as percent of GDP—will be approaching 100%. ...So what happens?

First, there really is no magical point when the world stops turning, like the 90-100% that is frequently quoted. Unfortunately, there are numerous countries now over 100%, and you guessed it, they are not doing very well. The best example is Japan at 200%, a result of Keynesian style fiscal spending over two decades of awful economic malaise.

However, there is a point that the debt must be addressed, and there are only a few options. We must address it because the bond market will demand it, through interest rates needed for investors to own the debt. We will look at the finances of Team USA in Chapter 12.

When the mound of debt larger than Charles Barkley's mid-section gets so high, there are only a few options: default, reform, or reflate.

DEFAULT

Default has all kinds of names that you would recognize, as we hear them all the time in our post-2008 world. Commonly heard terms such as "restructuring" and "recapitalization" simply sound kinder and gentler than "default." But in real life, they are the same thing. Monthly, we hear about Cyprus, Greece, Spain, or Portugal without a reference to "default," but never is a spade called a spade.

Excuse the CFA investment manager/professor for a moment, but when one values any investment, it is simply calculated as the present value of the cash flows plus the present value of the asset when you sell it or it matures. Both are discounted back by a rate that reflects the riskiness of the payer and the required rate of the return of the buyer. This has been true for ages; it is applicable to bonds, stocks, real estate, and all other investments.

Debt—whether for you, me, or even an entire country—is a bond. The two pieces of cash flow are the interest payments and the maturity value of the bond. Capitalism relies heavily on savers, investors, and trust, which is why it is called the bond market and is our country's largest market. A disruption, valuing an investment by defaulting, has some serious implications and a tremendously negative effect on the economy.

If the U.S. defaulted, it would cause a worldwide nightmare and a global depression.

When a country "restructures," the terms of the debt are changed materially by payment interruptions and/or extensions of the interest payments. It can also entail a change in the maturity date (make it longer and thereby worth less) or maturity amount. When you then calculate the present value—what it is worth right now—the restructuring costs the bondholder dearly. Typically, the investor loses 30 to 70 cents of every $1 invested. And no bond holder is smiling at that!

Default is the ugliest option out there. Repercussions would include a prolonged period of economic depression that could be as stark as the 1930s. It can, and eventually will, happen if steps are not taken to alter the current trajectory of debt driven by fiscal spending.

REFORM

Our chosen leaders' next option is to indeed lead and reform the system. In plain English, stop spending more than you take in and maybe even reverse the trend to chisel away at the mountain of debt. I'd like to name this option with three summarizing words: "Wake up America!"

The political process is so broken because the majority of people want something for free. The system enables more than half of Americans to receive some type of entitlement from the government. (We'll cover that in detail in Chapter 14.) And that is not sustainable. Pro-spending Keynesian economics is much more fun and much more politically attractive versus austerity and its spending cuts. To date, any American that would stand up and say, "I would invoke these cuts and really reform our outdated, outmoded structure" would be booed off the stage before the show even got started. So we punt, and kick the can down the road (to our kids and unborn grandkids), and focus on every political hot potato *except* Finance 101 and our bankrupt house.

The policymakers of choice—yes, our choice—do not appear to prefer fiscal responsibility. Big government is in style, further driving us toward the cliff. Reform... rest in peace.

I must opine that this second option, that of reform, is my preferred one without question.

Writing about Americans favoring big government is really difficult for me to do, and even more, very sad. I suspect any American milking the system, legally or illegally, will get the opportunity to spend some quality time in Hades.

REFLATE

The third and last option is the one we are attempting to perform. Much quieter politically and allowing the fiscal side to continue to get its failing grade, extremely loose monetary policy unfortunately looks like the chosen path. The more than quadrupling of the Fed balance sheet is an attempt to reflate our way out.

When the amount of money in circulation increases, inflation always follows, yet with a substantial lag of several years. We learned this in the 1960s and 1970s experiments, with the remedy occurring in 1980, with Volcker's restrictive policy and the associated super recessions of the early 1980s.

Reflating's primary purpose is to create inflation so effectively that debt repayment is cheaper. Every dollar buys a little less, and so does the cheaper dollar that you pay your debt with. Those of us who are old enough can remember the 1970s, when we earned $20,000 and an automobile cost $2,500. Fast-forward to today where our dollars are worth a lot less. Reflation is simply speeding up this process as inflation goes higher. The problem with this option is that the major entitlement programs are indexed to inflation, thus making the liabilities larger!

It blows me away thinking about what I have witnessed in my brief 55 years. We had this Keynesian economics thing, disproved it in practice and in theory; experienced runaway inflation and then remedied it (albeit a painful process); had an incredibly fun life and career because we adopted Reaganomics and the concept of incentives, low tax rates, and small government; had a Financial Crisis as a result of the housing boom/bust that was caused by too much regulation and a disrespect for the "invisible hand." And now we've fully embraced only the spending side of Keynesian economics and just changed the label on the package to Obamanomics! We have doubled our debt in less than five years with more coming every year in the foreseeable future. To add insult to injury, because of our debt, we are *praying* for inflation. Is that right?

Kind of makes you want to upchuck. To all in Washington, how silly is that paragraph above?

CHAPTER 10
THE FOLLY OF KEYNESIANISM

There is no such thing as a free lunch.

~ Milton Friedman
Economist & University of Chicago Professor

John Maynard Keynes remains one of the most influential economists of all time. Born in England in 1883, he was brilliant as well as extremely liberal. He was called on by the British government in World War I for his economic expertise. Keynes forewarned the government of the collapse of the Weimar Republic in Germany when France demanded compensation for destruction from the war and Germany simply printed the money.

Best known for *The General Theory of Employment, Interest and Money* that was published in 1936, Keynes argued that markets are inherently unstable, and interventionist policies are essential to tackling a recession and the associated unemployment. Keynes believed that aggregate demand—the sum of consumption and investment—needs a stimulus from government (e.g., public works projects) or unemployment would grow indefinitely high. Many countries adopted his work.

Keynesian economics really ascended in the following three to four decades. By the 1950s, Keynesianism was adopted worldwide, in the public sector and in universities alike. Included in the Keynesian thought process was the Philips Curve—a concept that states there is an inverse relationship between inflation and unemployment.

The largest challenger to this economic way of thinking was Austrian Frederic Hayek, whose prescription was to set the markets free and have little government intervention. Hayek said Keynes' beliefs suffered from "fatal conceit"—a belief that smart people can do the impossible. Milton Friedman was a huge fan of Hayek's, and further progressed the questioning of Keynesian theories. By the 1970s (when I first learned of the conflicting theories), criticisms abounded about Keynesianism. Why? As Pops used to look at me in a mystified way and say, "Cause it doesn't work!"

The 1970s witnessed stagflation—a period where we had both high and increasing inflation and unemployment. The Philips Curve? It didn't work either. More and more focus was on monetary policy and the importance of slow, steady, and predictable growth in the money supply rather than fiscal spending to revive the economy in cyclical downturns.

Our leaders now turn their heads to an important half of Keynes' theory. They have embraced (oh so convincingly) the first half—spend in downturns to prime the economic pump. But the other 50% of the equation—save when times are good—has purposely been ignored and the term 'surplus' is removed from the dictionary. The result is the huge and growing unsustainable debt levels.

Much of the questioning of Keynesian economics has been driven by what was experienced—how Keynesian theory performed outside the university and how the theories associated with the many aggregate demand charts and graphs performed.

When FDR came storming out of the gate with an experimental program known as the New Deal in 1933, many were relieved that the worst was over and the country would be looking up from that point on. The focus was threefold: relief for the poor and unemployed, recovery of the economy to normalcy, and reform to prevent a repeat of the deep recession.

Although not specifically labeled Keynesianism in 1933, the program had very similar elements to the teachings of Keynes.

Unemployment was truly the largest issue of the times, persisting at normal levels in the 1920s—about 5%—before soaring to nearly 25% in 1933. It remained above 15% until the start of World War II in 1941.

...What about the deficits associated with the New Deal?

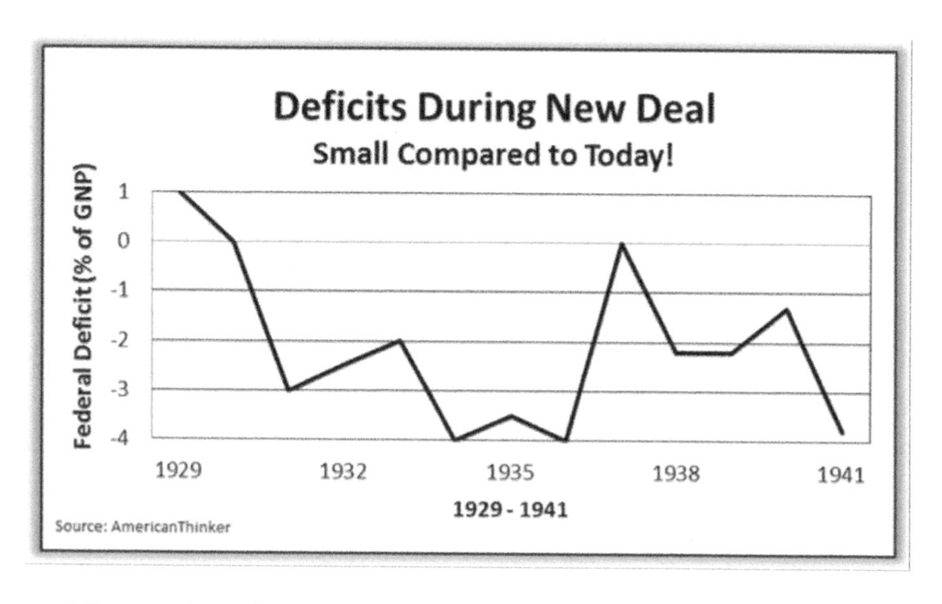

The surplus of 1929 gave way to deficits every year in the 1930s. The worst deficit years were approximately 4% in 1934-1936 and they averaged 2% over the entire time period. Proponents say the New Deal worked, evidenced by the return to a balanced budget in 1937. But as the charts illustrate, huge (at the time) deficit spending did not restore economic health, as unemployment remained very high by any era's standards.

Incidentally, most economists put the blame of the Depression on a reduction in the money supply.

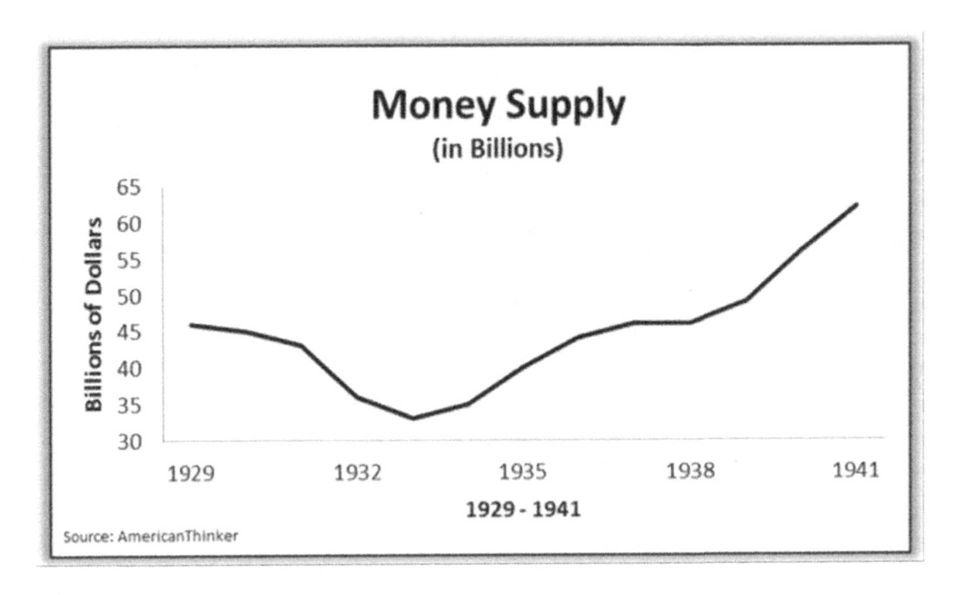

Little at the time was known about the money supply. Note how there was a significant contraction in the worst Depression years in 1929-1933. In addition, the velocity of money was incorrectly assumed to be constant, thereby further contributing to the pronounced economic slowdown.

By 1939, FDR's Treasury Secretary, Henry Morgenthau, quipped, "We have tried spending money. We are spending more than we've ever spent before and it does not work. ...After eight years of the Administration we have just as much unemployment as when we started—with an enormous debt to boot!" Debt had increased to over 20% of GDP in the 1930s.

With the benefit of hindsight, most students of economic history believe that FDR and the New Deal only prolonged the agony. He also added a flurry of new taxes. The incentives to invest and take risks by those who had any money were severely wounded.

If you believe in the power of prayer, and now you see the folly of Keynesianism, now might be time to say a rosary. Compare these philosophies and numbers to where we stand in 2014! What on earth are we doing? Can you say Pete and Repeat? …But this time, deficits are on steroids!!

Job growth can only return on the back of private investment, not government work projects that go away, leaving the private sector to pay the debt associated with the projects. If you get real job growth, you will get tax revenue.

So Keynesianism does not work. Interestingly, one of life's most ironic moments occurred ten days before Keynes' death on April 21, 1946. The great theorist recanted on his own deathbed! Quoth Keynes: "I find myself more and more relying for a solution of our problems on the invisible hand which I tried to eject from economic thinking twenty years ago."

What is the history of the other theories regarding fiscal policies? Below is my chart that covers nearly the last hundred years.

ERA	POLICY	SHORT DESCRIPTION	COMMENTS
1. Pre 1929	None	Balance the budget.	Economics field - 1st inning.
2. 1930s to 1960s	Keynesian	"Prime the Pump" in recession. Run surpluses in expansions.	Countercyclical policy.
3. 1970s	Crowding Out	Deficits = higher interest rates, decline in investments, and exports.	Common sense, but short-lived.
4. 1970s	Neo-Classical	Deficit spending offset by fear of higher taxes.	True, but never gained much traction.
5. 1980s	Supply-Side Economics / Reaganomics	Lower rates = higher revenue. Minimal gov't and regulation. Incentives matter!	Laffer inspired; success "trickles down."
6. 2008 to ?	Obamanomics	Gov't spending cures all. Higher tax rates. Redistributionist. Debt doubling+ is OK.	Shame on success. Pay a "fair share." Keynesian II... but worse!

First, note there have not been many economic theories. We were shocked by the Depression, thus Keynes' ascent. We then realized Keynesian economics didn't work. Subsequently, for a short period of time, we debated "Crowding Out" and "Neo-Classical" theories. Importantly, what we learned as we all matured in the field of economics is that there was this item called "expectations" that made many of the theories—including Keynesian—ineffective and questionable to use going forward.

Along came Art Laffer, Ronald Reagan, and Paul Volcker… and thankfully Keynesianism went six feet under. Done. Buried. Not even

Lazarus could rise from being that dead. Incentives work! Low marginal tax rates drive the businessman's thinking (you'll never talk me out of that one!) and tax revenues are in abundance.

But the Crisis occurred, and times have changed. How many times do we have to get our heads close to the mule before we realize it kicks? A reversion to a disproved theory is at hand—with a sparking fuse getting shorter by the minute!

A May 5th, 2013 article in the *New York Times Magazine* highlighted the theories of Larry Summers, former Director of the White House Office of Management and Budget until 2010 and the former president of Harvard. His Keynesian philosophy, even after all the lack of success, includes the promotion of more government spending (he helped design the $800 billion 2009 stimulus package) with more infrastructure to assist the long-term unemployed. His philosophy vehemently denies the disincentives of higher taxes, and thinks inheritance taxes should be higher, as wealth is "problematic" in a society committed to freedom of opportunity. Mr. Summers was a leading candidate to replace Fed Chairman Bernanke but he pulled his candidacy, and the markets applauded loudly. Do you get the picture on these outmoded, free-spending minds?

I must apologize and I'll opine a loud disagreement that is very representative of my business friends, as follows. The long-term unemployed are there because we have incented them to be there, à la Europe (where the natural rate of unemployment is significantly higher). People like me, who have created jobs in the real world (not just wrote academic papers) have been hit with much higher tax rates and expectations and we will be hit again. Our tolerance for dealing with growing big government is waning! And lastly, the disincentives associated with inheritance taxes for a successful entrepreneur—because you want to tax successful entrepreneurism just once more "on our way out"—is socialistic.

The vendetta to penalize the successful through higher taxes just does not move the deficit/debt needles. It is very disheartening. Heightened uncertainty is the ultimate villain for investment. And government investment does not create permanent jobs.

Due to the Financial Crisis of 2007-2009, the power of free markets that unleashed the incredible economic period beginning in 1982 is now in question. Most of today's policymakers in power believe that the free markets need to be reined in! Regulate! Spend to prime da pump! Liberal bureaus say we should do more and more. And if that does not work... do more!

What we have today is worse than Keynesianism. The theory of Keynes included a need to stimulate economic growth in recessions. To accomplish this, policymakers increased government spending and decreased tax rates. In contrast, our current policymakers also believe that we need to stimulate economic growth in a recessionary period, and they increase government spending like Keynes, but they *increase* tax rates! The effect of higher tax rates—feeling the impact AND fearing even higher rates—more than offsets government spending. Today's policy simply favors a huge government sector and a smaller private sector.

Sadly, what we have learned about the role of expectations and incentives has all been thrown out the door. The empirical evidence of the beneficial effects from Keynesian-like stimulus plans does not exist. And history suggests (O, Canada) the opposite may be true. The majority of economists believe so. Only the redistributionist liberal ones pull out the Keynesian card. And most forget, or choose to forget, it never worked nor will it ever work. That's what I mean by the folly of Keynesianism.

CHAPTER 11
A TALE OF TWO COUNTRIES

Canada is a good country to be from. It has a gentler, slower pace—it lends perspective.

~ Paul Anka
Canadian-American Singer & Actor

We understand the reason solid GDP growth has a huge impact on our personal lives, as well as the health of our country. Solid growth improves our standard of living and is necessary to provide the revenue needed to generate funds to allow the government to fund its spending.

We get solid GDP growth only when we have both sound fiscal and monetary policy. We have seen the ill effects of bad policies including no monetary knowledge in the 1930s, too easy money with too much regulation (the Houses for Everyone Syndrome in the 2000s), and leverage prior to the 2007 crash.

We have also witnessed periods of great prosperity, led by the 1980s through 2000. Influential policies included fiscal responsibility, sound monetary policy, minimal regulation, low tax rates that incentivized people to produce, and thus, much tax revenue. The result was solid GDP growth. We achieved low and controlled inflation, low unemployment, and maintenance of the debt as percent of GDP to a desirable 30% to 40%.

Before we take a look at the current status of our nation in the next part of this book, let's briefly look at the role important policies have played in the last few decades with two of our allies and largest trading partners—Japan and Canada.

JAPAN

Japan experienced an incredible economic period commencing in 1960. Sound policies resulted in an amazing 6% GDP growth rate, which resulted in income levels growing commensurate with the U.S. A bubble in the housing and stock market developed in the late 1980s, predictably leading to defaults and banking problems, and resulted in a slow GDP growth rate. Stocks rose 400% in the five years from 1984 to 1989, and then retreated over the next 25 years to its 1984 levels—75% off the highs of 1989.

The Japanese employed a Keynesian style fiscal policy. They went all-in on infrastructure spending, and ran deficits of 5-7% per year. Sound a tad familiar? Did government spending bureaucrats spur GDP growth? Predictably, no—and the national debt of Japan ballooned.

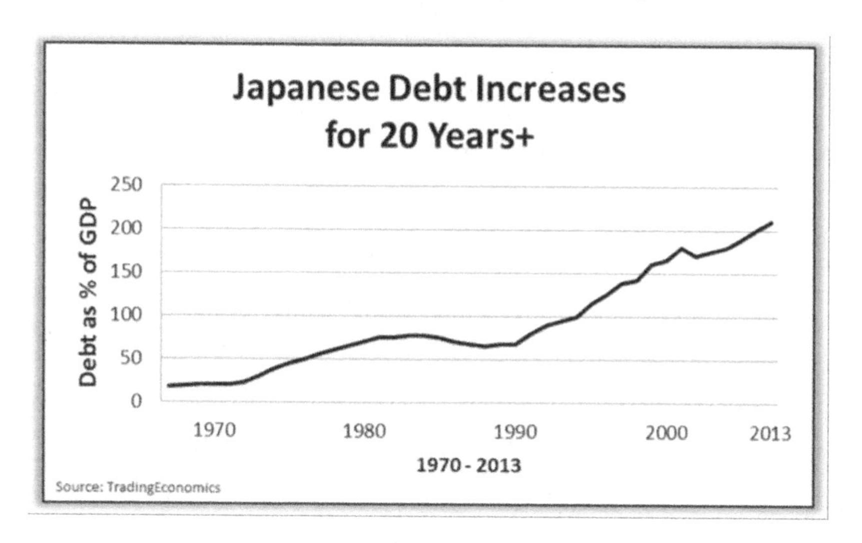

Note the ascent of the debt as percent of GDP from 70% in the early and mid-1980s to over 200% today.

So fiscal responsibility was ignored, and the stimulus did not work. What of monetary policy? Japan decreased the rate of growth of the money supply from double digits to just 2-3%. The result was deflation and stagnant

GDP growth for a generation. Also influential was (and still is) the aging demographics, where the elder portion of the population grew profoundly. The increased costs of retirement and medical needs called for higher tax rates, which invariably resulted in slower GDP growth. Downright ugly.

In summary, wrong fiscal policy with lots of spending and debt, plus a restrictive monetary policy, resulted in an extended period of economic malaise. In addition, a failure to address an aging population helped in developing a bleak future for the next generations in Japan.

Not until 2013 did Japan change its course regarding economic policies. They finally have adopted a more monetarist philosophy, are running the printing presses, and have adopted a 2% inflation target.

CANADA

Canada, you may say, is either a little smarter or a little ahead of the curve relative to the U.S. and Europe.

Prior to the mid-1990s, Canada was running very large deficits at both the federal and state/province level.

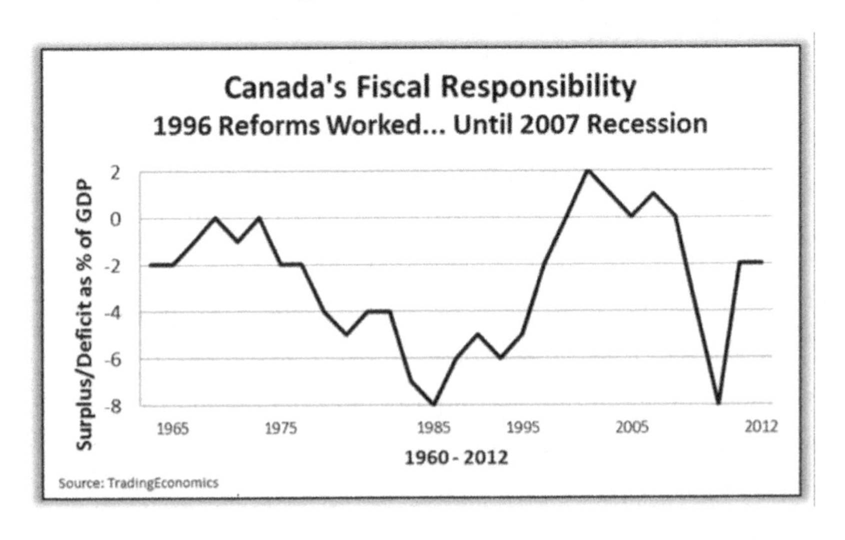

Note that Canada closed its deficits in a few short years with the reforms in 1996. A real display of austerity and a swallowing of the pill for years of not taking care of themselves was the prescription.

And the debt as percent of GDP fell consistently from over 100% to nearly 60% before the Great Recession in the U.S., which affected Canada as one of our largest trading partners.

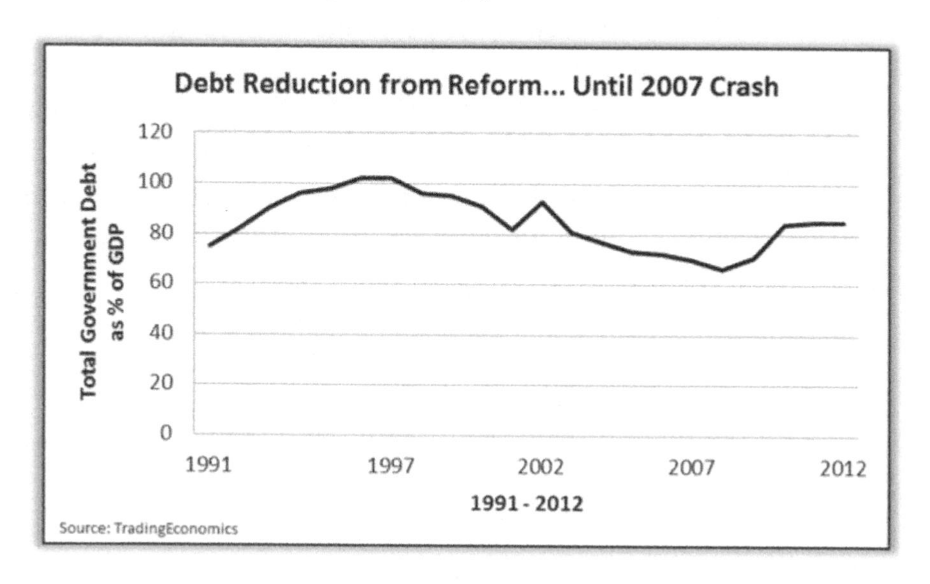

So if the debt went way down and I am a Keynesian, then I could be certain that GDP had to suffer miserably, right?

Sorry, Johnny. GDP growth rate in the ten years following the 1996 policy changes was a very palatable 3% annual rate. This is another vivid illustration that the teachings of Keynes are incorrect. GDP growth was half that rate with the huge deficits. And after the 1996 changes, unemployment fell dramatically. Now that's called getting your house in order! Again: *O Canada!*

Canada is one of the great success stories and an illustration of how good leaders lead. Work hard, pay the bills, spend only what you have, stop putting your hand out, enjoy life and your position in it, and decrease big government, à la Ronald Reagan.

A brief few words on the recent success of Britain seem appropriate at this moment. Since the coalition government was appointed in 2010 as recognition of a national crisis, the structural deficit has been reduced by over 4%, and importantly with 80% derived from spending cuts and 20% from a sales tax increase. Economic growth has increased as has job creation. The Brits even plan on running surpluses in good times. HARK!

I have included the plights of these countries to compare and contrast the tales of them as well as to GIVE YOU HOPE! We honestly do know there are proven economic policies—both ones that work and ones that are fallacies. The fallacies need to be undressed to show their truest form and color, as many are currently dressed with deceptive "other-agenda" clothes. And the hourglass is getting bottom heavy…

PART III.
AN ANALYSIS OF TEAM USA

In Part IV, we take a good, hard look at the finances of Team USA, including revenues and expenses during the last 15 years as well as the trends characteristic of both. We'll look at the major programs that drive these trends and explain how we got where we are.

Entitlement trends are highlighted, and we analyze and score Team USA on the key fiscal policy variables. A description of the many head-winds is presented along with my proposal for some common sense policies that could alter the unattractive trends of the most important economic variables.

CHAPTER 12
ANALYZING THE FINANCIAL STATEMENTS

Your net worth to the world is usually determined by what remain after your bad habits are subtracted from your good ones.

~ Benjamin Franklin
Founding Father of the United States

Before investing in any company, industry, or country, successful investors typically "test the temperature of the water"—where the potential investment is located and how the business is operated.

As a Chartered Financial Analyst (CFA) and money manager for three decades, I have always been a firm believer in looking first at the macroeconomic environment—the old "which way is the wind blowing" test. How are the fundamentals of the economy? How is monetary policy being handled? What is the status from a fiscal prudence perspective?

Second, valuation is important. There are numerous useful valuation metrics, but the simplest and best is the Price earnings ratio level of the overall market. There are several other quite useful indicators.

Third, I remain a true believer in technical analysis. Charts of data that assist you in detecting important trends and foretell timely entry and exit points can prove to be extremely useful.

Only after looking at the fundamentals, valuation, and technicals of the environment does one's good, old-fashioned fundamental analysis of the company provides perspective.

So what about investing in the stock of our country—let's call it Team USA? Mary Meeker, former Wall Street prophet and now Kleiner Perkins strategist, did an excellent job (first in early 2011) of analyzing Team USA by providing a basic summary of America's financial statements. Many of my thoughts on this topic are attributable to this study with the data and graphs updated to more current (and yes uglier) numbers.

Whether you are viewing three year-old or current day data, the financials are downright alarming. America is a company I would not touch with a ten-foot pole. We have spent ourselves into a gaping, dark hole. Let's look at the specifics of Team USA.

First and foremost, bear with me as the nerdy Certified Public Accountant (CPA) in me spews forth. Financial statements tell most of the story. They summarize how successfully one is delivering on their mission statement. The income statement reveals how they are doing in the current year and the balance sheet is the accumulation of all prior years and the source of strength to accomplish the company's goals.

Team USA's financial statements are not looking too pretty. They are in deep trouble. There are trends that could make you sick. We've covered the all-important annual deficit as percent of GDP in Chapter 7.

Let's look at the sources of revenues and expenses for fiscal year 2011.

Fiscal 2011 USA			
REVENUE	**Billion $**	**% Total Revenue**	
Individual Income Tax	1,091	47%	
Social Security Tax	819	36%	
Other (Duties/Fees)	212	9%	
Corporate Income Tax	181	8%	
TOTAL			**$ 2,303**
EXPENSES	**Billion $**	**% Total Revenue**	
Medicare & Medicaid	761	21%	
Social Security	731	20%	
Defense	706	20%	
Discretionary (Education, Infrastructure, Law)	650	18%	
Unemployment	526	15%	
Net Interest	230	6%	
TOTAL			**$ 3,604**
		NET LOSS/DEFICIT	**-1,301**
		% OF REVENUE	**56%**
Source: White House Office of Management & Budget			

Ladies and gentlemen, how long would you stay in business if your expenses of $3,603 billion are 50% higher than your revenue of $2,303 billion? Not for very long.

Things have improved since fiscal year 2011, but one must ask how much and what are the reasons for the improvements and then compare the numbers to longer term trends.

It is helpful to look at revenues and expenses over the last 15 years, as well as surpluses and deficits as percent of GDP. The chart below shows data from this period beginning in 1997, running through the fiscal year ending September 30, 2013.

Revenue and Spending the Last 15 Years					
Year	GDP (Billions)	Revenue	Spending	Surplus/ Deficit	% of GDP
1998	8,793	1,721	1,652	69	1
1999	9,353	1,827	1,702	125	1
2000	9,951	2,025	1,789	236	2
2001	10,286	1,991	1,862	129	1
2002	10,642	1,853	2,010	(157)	-1
2003	11,142	1,782	2,160	(378)	-3
2004	11,853	1,880	2,292	(412)	-3
2005	12,623	2,153	2,472	(319)	-3
2006	13,377	2,406	2,655	(249)	-2
2007	14,029	2,568	2,728	(160)	-1
2008	14,369	2,524	2,982	(458)	-3
2009	13,939	2,105	3,518	(1,413)	-10
2010	14,736	2,102	3,456	(1,354)	-9
2011	15,321	2,680	3,662	(982)	-6
2012	15,777	2,450	3,540	(1,090)	-7
2013	16,585	2,774	3,454	(680)	-4
Source: Congressional Budget Office					

When I first saw this chart, I was amazed and distraught. The shaded areas in the far right column represent the deficits as percent of GDP. This really highlights the good first five years versus the ugly last five years. These numbers are the result of solid economic policies versus ones I categorize as suspect.

Several observations come to light. First is the incredibly large dollar amount of the deficits in recent years, seen shaded in the surplus/deficit column. We have had a near trillion-dollar deficit in four of the last five years, averaging a whopping 7% of GDP. In total, this is over a $5.5 trillion deficit increase, cumulatively exceeding 35% of GDP. It took us 200-plus years to increase our debt to 35% of GDP, and we've doubled our debt to over 70% in a few short years!

Next, look at the recovering revenue figures, as 2011 and 2012 are back to previous highs, and 2013 was a record revenue year. Then look at the expense dollar figures. They increased 40% from $2.5 trillion in 2005 to $3.5 trillion in 2009—and holding steady! And we aren't having a spending problem?

The revenue increase is a function of the tax rate increases, the end of the payroll tax holiday, and accelerated capital gains that occurred in late 2012 as investors realized gains at the lower rate and paid them in 2013. I would not expect the coming years to see such increases as most of us adjust to higher rates.

The data can also be analyzed from looking at both revenue and spending trends as percent of GDP.

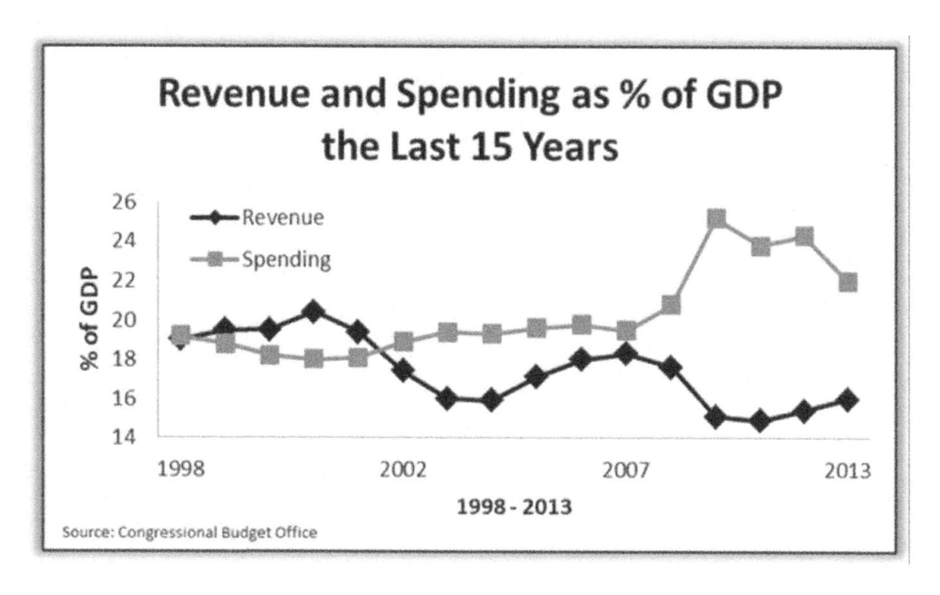

The annual growth rate of spending is higher than the annual growth rate of revenue. That's not good. Revenue growth has kept pace with GDP growth over longer periods of time, but struggled in the Great Recession, as the world seemed to stop turning. Economic growth drives revenue, but you will get neither if you raise tax rates. I am for closing many loopholes, but never have been (nor ever will be) for rate increases—they kill incentives instantly! Observe the first five years, where revenue was approximately 20% of GDP and we maintained our Clinton-esque spending in the 18-19% area. Hark! A surplus!

On the other hand, the current gap between revenues and expenses—averaging approximately 8% the last five years—has never been seen in peacetime American history. We just cannot keep spending like this—and how we're projected to in the future!

The CBO studied how fast GDP would have to grow to eliminate the deficit. They found that we need an unachievable 6-7% growth rate per year for about three years, followed by 4-5% in subsequent years.

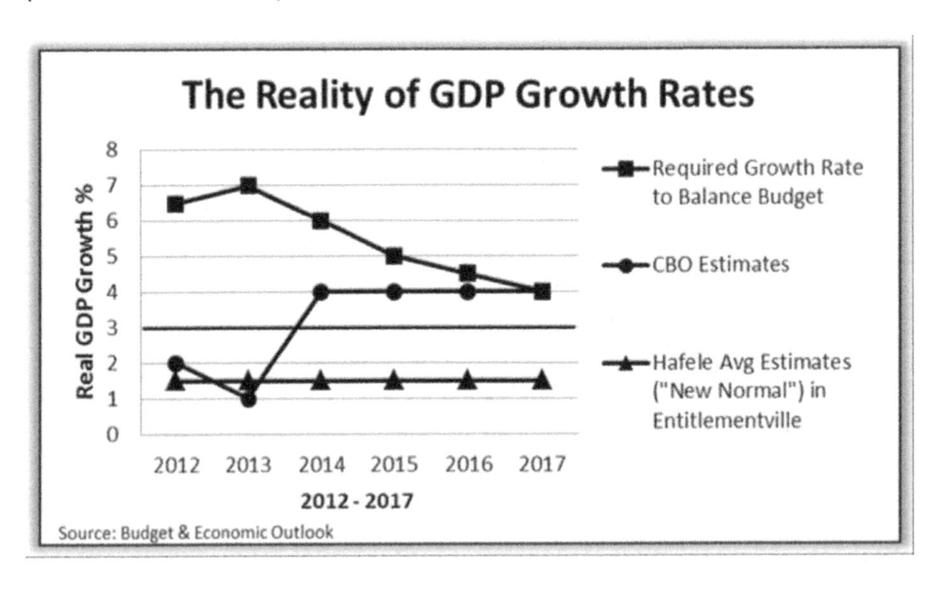

Something, ladies and gentlemen, is not right on the revenue or spending side if that's the case. And raising rates slows growth—common sense tells everyone that! That leaves cutting spending as the only remedy.

I have estimated, along with many others I follow in the investment business, that real GDP growth rates in the "new normal" environment of entitlements will be approximately 1.5% annually. Note the differences between what growth rate is required to balance the budget and what the CBO estimates. Also note the long-term average and my estimate. Somebody is downright wrong or simply not telling the truth.

The size of the government has grown substantially over the last 80 years.

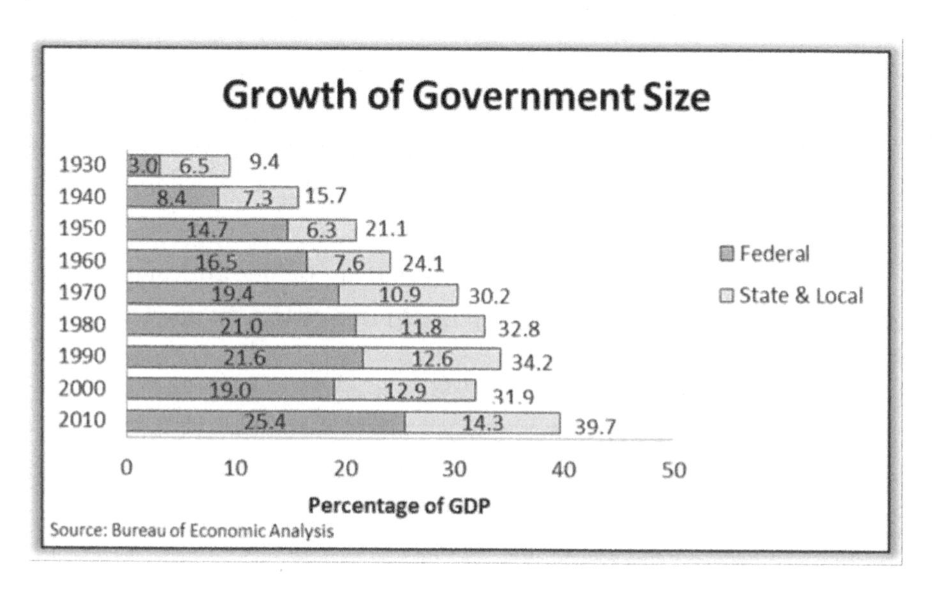

Each decade, government grew 3-5% of GDP until it leveled off in the low 30% area in 1970. Government actually shrunk as a percent of GDP in the 1990s—the function of a growing and fun economic period. But look at the growth to almost 40% by 2010. Those who do not think we have a growing government or a spending problem just ignore the facts and these numbers.

Entitlements are called transfer payments, and the growth of them at both the federal and state levels is noteworthy.

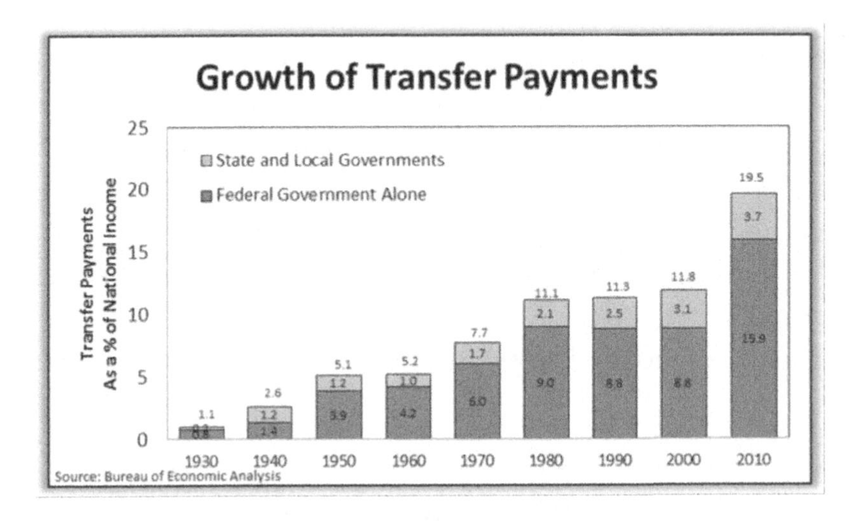

As percent of national income, transfer payments have skyrocketed. In the decade ending in 2010, they increased from 11.8% to 19.5%. That is a nearly a 65% increase in just ten years!

The changing role of government—getting bigger and bigger—can best be explained by analyzing defense and entitlement spending over the last fifty years.

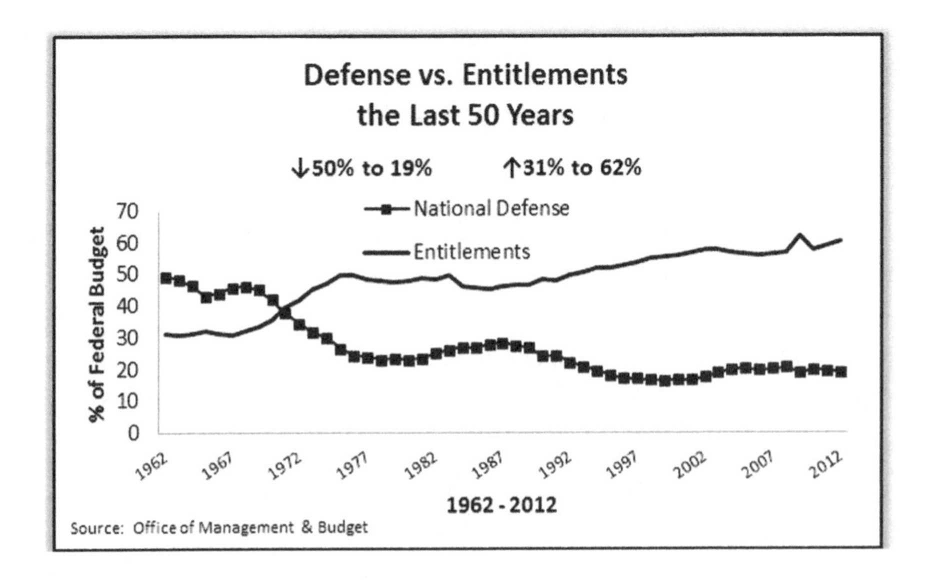

Over the last fifty years, defense has decreased from approximately half of the federal budget to less than 20%. On the other hand, entitlements have risen from less than a third to 62%!

Speaking of government programs, we must address Social Security, Medicare, and Medicaid. By far, they are the largest entitlements. Combined, they eat up the majority of the budget (Social Security about half of that, Medicare and Medicaid the other half). Yet less than a third of Americans think any reductions are appropriate. Amazing!

In summary, the arithmetic speaks volumes. The financial statements and trends are not very attractive. And why our leaders prefer to focus on everything but these numbers is beyond me and most of my colleagues.

CHAPTER 13
HOW WE GOT HERE

The best minds are not in government. If any were, business would hire them away.

~ Ronald Reagan

I think it is helpful to contrast this generation's Roaring 20s-like period in the late 1990s with this most recent period of the Financial Crisis. These eras are at the extreme right and extreme left of the fun meter. The comparison illustrates just how we got into this mess we are in today. But let's look at the long-term picture, just to confirm that we are not blowing this thing out of proportion.

Below are revenues and expenses as percent of GDP since 1900.

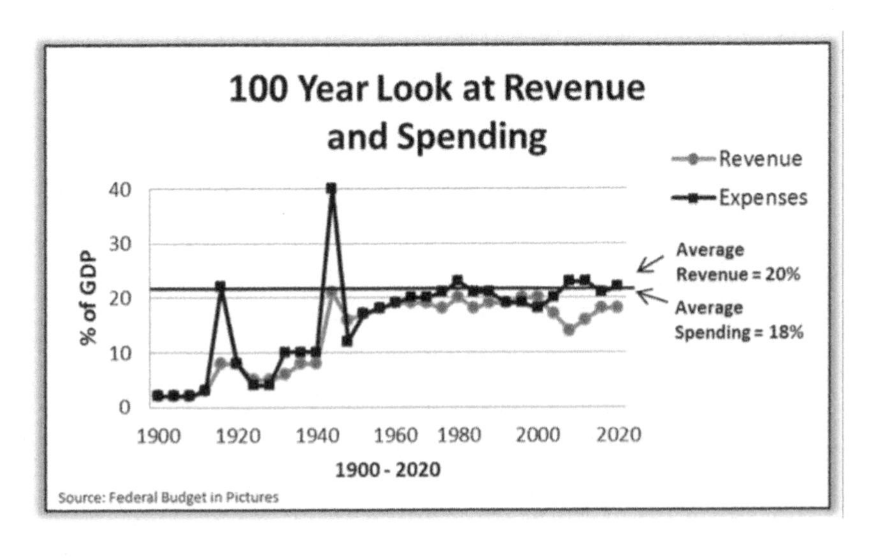

First, notice that for a century, the leaders of our country have been fiscally prudent—the revenue and expense lines stay close together. Just like our parents taught us: watch our spending relative to our income! The notable exception is the early 1940s when we, by necessity, were appropriately spendthrift for combat infrastructure in our successful accomplishment of defending capitalism. Another interesting point of this graph is that total government spending was less than 5% of GDP in 1930.

Second, note the small gap in the 1970s and 1990s, where we spent 2-3% more than revenue generated. We got comfortable running small deficits under the theory it was okay as long as GDP was growing 2-4%! If so, the cumulative debt as percent of GDP would remain steady or even decrease.

But look at the current gap—the widest in peacetime history.

Check out those enviable four years commencing in 1997, when revenue exceeded expenses (hard to see but oh so pretty). I still get goose bumps thinking of those days! All the fun, the business success, and frolicking with my beautiful daughters as they blossomed into fine young ladies.

So what in the world are we doing spending so much money? My father, a WWII Navy Vet, and still going pretty strong at 90, best describes this phenomenon as "spending like a drunken sailor." The major programs including Social Security (1935), welfare (1935), Medicare and Medicaid (1965), education subsidies (1965), and a few others, account for over 40% of government spending.

All in all, the progression of government has occurred in many of the primary areas of our economy—housing, retirement, healthcare, finance, energy, education, and more. Some is good, some is bad. But in the aggregate, government is growing too much and has become too big! Put your political preferences aside and the arithmetic does not lie!

Spending has increased too dramatically, and most of it is entitlement spending, driven by the aging of America and the associated healthcare and retirement benefits. We have failed miserably in predicting the magnitude of these programs and the effect they have created on incentives.

Entitlement spending is about $16,000 per household. Consequently, people no longer practice self-reliance; saving for the future and retirement is non-existent for many Americans. Why? We are instilled with the mentality that Uncle Sam will take care of us, which encourages dependence. Are these perverse incentives or what? Other countries support 20% savings rates, and ours have been ridiculously low, single-digit rates for some time now.

These policies might be defensible if they produced results, but they don't. Let's look at some possible solutions to these problems.

SOCIAL SECURITY

Social Security is easily fixed with solid leadership.

Created in 1935, it's a pay-as-you-go system that acts as an intergenerational income transfer program, and is heavily influenced by demographics. It is appropriately described as a Ponzi scheme. In 1950, there were over 15 workers per recipient, and the life expectancy of a 65-year old (the established age for retirement in the U.S.) was somewhere between 1 and 2 years. Party on, Gramps! Fast-forward to today, there are about three workers paying into Social Security for every recipient, with a forecast of two workers by 2030.

The problem is the life expectancy of a 65-year old is now over 15 years. So compare 1935, when 30 workers paid in for one recipient for 1-2 years, to two workers paying in for one recipient for over 15 years—the Ponzi scheme tilts!

As the boomers retire and the population over 65 grows rapidly, the projected benefits far outweigh the projected receipts from taxes.

The shortfalls, called "unfunded liabilities," are mind-boggling. It is about half the size of our economy. And Medicare is even worse on this front. Put together, these two programs are approximately three times the size of GDP. The real problem is the demographics.

Fixes include a combination of the following options, as each has pros and cons, thus proponents and opponents:

1. Cut benefits: increase the retirement age, lower the benefit formula, minimize the cost of living adjustments (COLA), and invoke "means testing" (where the rich get zero benefits).

2. Increase taxes: raise the tax ceiling, raise the tax rate (be careful!).

3. Alter disincentives to work, which are part of the program.

Other inappropriate ways to fix the program include cutting spending in other areas and borrowing, both of which seem to be politically unacceptable.

The structure is outdated and we somehow need to make people save for their own retirement. We need a 401(k)-like plan to be phased in, providing incentives for people to work and mandatorily save for one's retirement.

The sooner we make the necessary changes, the better off we'll be. But the leveraging of America and the associated very low savings rate promote caution, as some 50% of recipients sadly have no other source of income when they retire.

MEDICARE and MEDICAID

The Medicare program is funded with a 2.9% payroll tax, split evenly between employer and employee. To fix it, projections show the rate needs to be a whopping 6.8%—another 3.9% increase out of your and my paychecks. Oh, no! Obamacare II with yet another 4% tax increase. So there really is only one option—benefits must be reduced significantly.

For years, I have told the story about my wonderful late mother, Shirley, regarding Medicare costs. Struggling greatly in the last few years of her eighties, she would go to three doctors weekly. And guess how much she paid every visit? Not a nickel. Medicare paid it all. Would she, or her doctors, deem those weekly visits essential if she had to pay out of her pocket? An excellent remedy is to convert to some amount of annual benefits with accumulated features like health savings accounts.

Medicaid, unlike its two sisters, Social Security and Medicare, goes to the poor and does not have a funding source. So it's the worst by design in terms of sustainability or accountability of the program.

All in all, our current healthcare programs incent us to consume, while Team USA foots the bill. The demographic driver of healthcare is the same one driving Social Security. They need to be carefully examined in order to alter these programs to suit the reality of our country's crumbling economic landscape.

Government healthcare costs are a function of these two 1965 Great Society programs, intended to assist the elderly and the poor. Medicare was intended to assist 10% of Americans and Medicaid 2%. Fast-forward nearly fifty years and those numbers tilt to 15% and 16%, respectfully. The result is that government spending on healthcare is about 8% of GDP, compared to 1% at the inception of the programs. Government programs grow and grow because the money they spend is not their own. It's free! No wonder our healthcare costs in the U.S. are approaching 20% of GDP and are 50-100% higher than all other developed countries. Yet we still have the same mortality rate—which means we get nothing for all those costs.

And it's about to get worse from a financial perspective. The Patient Protection and Affordable Care Act (ACA) is upon us and will insure an additional 10% of the population, or 30 million Americans. There is no increase in supply of doctors and hospitals to meet this increase in demand. A major change is just around the corner and I cannot fathom its effect on the deficit. People are afraid to quantify it and when they do, the press won't print it. As implementation requirements drew closer to the deadline of January 2014, the impact became clearer and some of the deadlines were extended a year. To make matters worse, the rollout of the ACA website sadly can only be described as a debacle. Sounds like complete confusion to me!

ACHIEVERS and RECEIVERS

Mother Shirley preached that there would always be achievers and receivers—and life's givers are so much more rewarded than the takers. So how many achievers and receivers are there now and what's the trend?

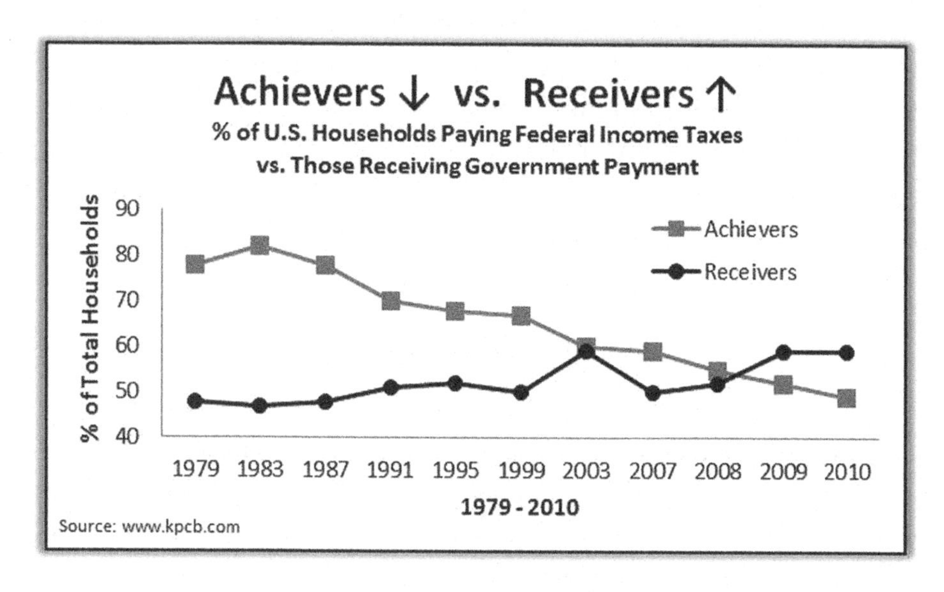

Well, I love you Mom and I still agree that giving makes people happier. But I am starting to feel like a relic.

In the 1980s era, the data shows that about four out of five American households paid federal income taxes. About 25 years ago, a descent commenced down to the current day level of under 50%. Half of America does not pay federal income taxes! And those receiving government-paid benefits (including Social Security, Medicare and Medicaid, education and energy assistance, unemployment compensation, subsidized housing, food stamps, earned income credit, and more) have soared. An incredible 59% of the population now receives government payments. Fifty-nine percent! In comparison, that number was approximately 20% in the mid-1960s.

Now some indeed deserve government payments. For example, most of us have paid in thousands of dollars annually for Social Security and it only seems right to get something back. But nearly 60% are receivers? Whoa! How can Team USA have less than half the people pay for all the products and services, and 60% not lift a finger?

Note the current gap in the lines—receivers are outnumbering achievers.

So we have gradually changed from 80% Achievers / 20% Receivers to about 40% Achievers / 60% Receivers, in just a handful of decades. Have we reached the tipping point? The current trajectories of expense line items makes a CFA analyzing Team USA cry out, "Run, Forrest, run!" We clearly need to change the trajectory before there is literally nothing left to give. But can we?

GOVERNMENT GONE WILD

The sixth century B.C. sage, Lao Tzu (literally meaning "Old Master" in Chinese), wrote the *Tao Te Ching*—the second most translated book in world literature. This work was very influential throughout the ages, especially among thinkers and practitioners of Buddhism and Confucianism. My favorite verse from this seminal philosopher's text is verse 75:

> *When taxes are too high, people go hungry.*
> *When government is too intrusive, people lose their spirit.*
> *Act for the people's benefit; trust them; leave them alone.*

This wisdom is over 2,500 years old. The spirit of the verse will never die!

Government spending as a percentage of the economy has become approximately seven times the size it was 100 years ago. Where are we going now? With spending at 22% or more, our debt will triple in the next twenty years (using some very optimistic GDP growth rates and very low interest rates on the debt) to beyond the tipping point, equaling approximately 150% of GDP.

Entitlement spending growth is the driver. That, along with interest expense, will exceed revenue by 2025, per the CBO.

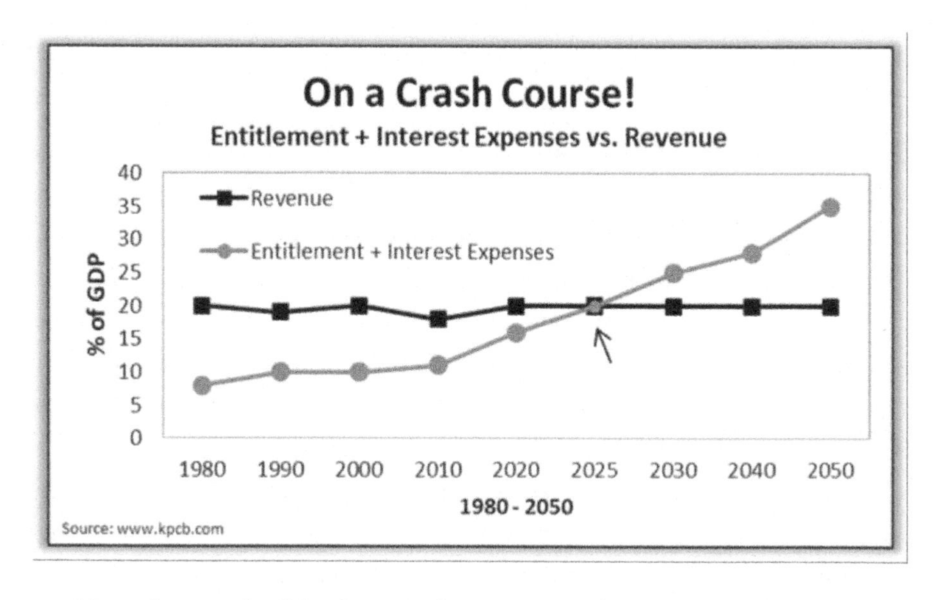

Note the trend of the lines—there is growth in spending yet again!

It seems we have changed our focus to what sounded good—a free lunch for everybody—departing from a system that actually worked.

On the revenue side, the largest tax breaks are healthcare premium deductibility, mortgage interest, accelerated depreciation, capital gain rates, charitable deductions, and 401(k) plans. If you eliminated all of them, most of the deficit would disappear. This would be a major change in our economy, commonly called a "sea change" due to the large amount of changes in the most influential economic drivers. The effects of any changes to these tax breaks that encourage investment could be incredibly negative on GDP.

A fact that should never be overlooked is the fact that the Achievers indeed are also the recipients of government benefits! The workers still get social security, law enforcement and use of the great infrastructure of the USA. However, the number of achievers becoming receivers for whatever reason one believes, simply cannot support the growth of government spending.

The Simpson-Bowles Commission issued their excellent report about three years ago. I have every MBA student in my classes study the details. The executive summary is that we can sensibly right the ship if we act now. In five to ten years, it will be beyond too late. And yes, the crash will be driven by the demographics applied to the existing dinosaur entitlement programs that dominate spending. Add interest costs to the rising debt and revenue is consumed. No more new schools, roads, or infrastructure. As John Mauldin eloquently described in his book *Endgame*—"BANG!" The entire economy pops and thus the "Great American Reset"!

I have often argued with some fairly astute comrades on the spending versus revenue issue. One of my friends who was also raised upper-lower class and rose to the CEO role has turned so liberal and sounds so uninformed that I cannot even talk with him about the financial world of today. He has been brainwashed by the partial truth-tellers.

The fact is over long periods of time, we have kept pace by raising the revenue with GDP growth, both at enviable 3% annual growth rates. This allowed low inflation, a palatable natural rate of unemployment, and a responsible level of debt.

Yet entitlement spending has grown at a 5% annual rate over the same forty years and now absorbs over 50% of expenses. Entitlements that are 2% higher than revenue per year mounts up after a few decades, and the acceleration of entitlements during the last few years has been breathtaking. Those who say we do not have a spending problem do not know the arithmetic or choose not to recognize the numbers. Nothing personal. Nothing political. Nothing anything. It is the arithmetic and they need to educate themselves. My children's futures are at stake!

GROW YOUR WAY OUT

Without question, raising the annual growth rate of GDP is the best way to address our deficits, and thereby reduce the debt. That would be the most essential element to reversing the downhill trajectory of Team USA.

How do you do that? We've discussed the Laffer Curve and the incentivizing nature of lowering tax rates that will result in increased revenues. Yet with the pile of debt growing, the world's appetite to try this (à la the successful Reaganomics experiment in the early 1980s), is unfortunately rather low.

Productivity gains played a viable and enviable way in the Internet era and earlier. Increases in productivity were a function of investments, and entitlements and government spending are not investments. If we rein in entitlements, we would have more money in the free market for investments, research, and development—endeavors in the private sector that create jobs.

CREATE AN AWARENESS

What can we do to "right the ship"? First, and the major impetus for why I wrote this book, is to create awareness—exposing today's true scorecard—of the magnitude and reality of the issue. It is paramount that everybody knows it is legal to alter the programs of Social Security, Medicare, and Medicaid. It is also moral to do so!

Second, we need real leadership! History illustrates for Team USA that there are numerous times where political and philosophical beliefs are cast aside to allow the real issues to be addressed. Financial vitality is the foundation for delivering any and all products and services. For some reason, our leaders don't seem to realize that Team USA is losing its competitive edge. Instead, they prefer to focus on other items that do *not* address the true scorecard.

BIG GOVERNMENT: GOOD OR BAD?

Government has become a very large and growing part of our economy. Is that good or bad?

The answer to that question can be addressed with another simple question: Does the size of government increase or decrease our quality of life? If so, how much effect does it have? In other words, does government size really influence per capita GDP growth rates?

Below is a graph of GDP growth rates of 23 developed countries for the 50-year period from 1960 to 2010.

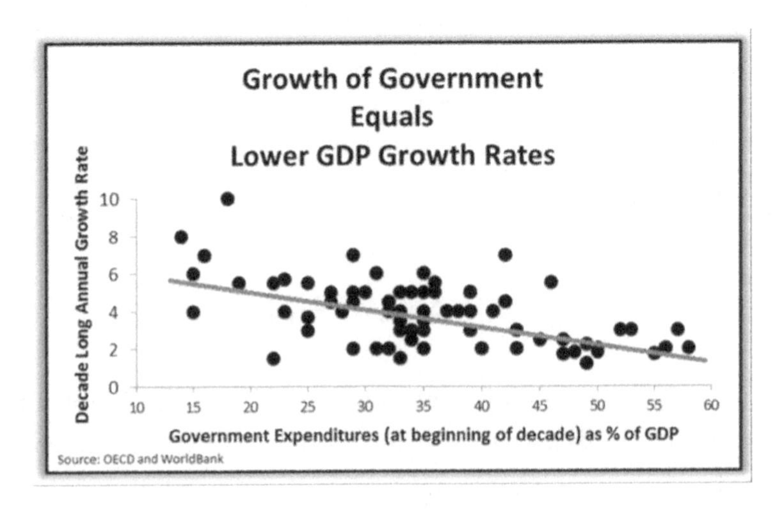

Each dot represents a ten-year period of economic growth of a single country and the size of government for that same country at the start of the decade. The observations tell us, collectively through using a multiple regression analysis, that there is a downward sloping line, which illustrates that as government gets larger, GDP growth slows. Thus, the quality of our lives does not increase as government gets larger. It actually decreases! This is a really important concept!

Economists from almost all schools of capitalism formerly agreed the optimal size of government is somewhere around 30-35% of GDP. The most socialist European states all linger around 50% to 55%, and have, not surprisingly, lower GDP growth rates. GDP growth rates are the best way to measure quality of life over long periods of time.

This graph illustrates that for a 10% increase in government expenditures as a percent of GDP, the growth rate is lowered by approximately 1%. If we socialize medicine, which is 18% of GDP, our growth rate would be reduced conservatively by approximately 1.5%. This means we could soon be down to about zero... Does that present a pause?

The size of government in many areas has skyrocketed. I recommend www.governmentgonewild.org if you're in the mood for shaking your head in puzzlement and disbelief. Total cost of a government employee versus one from the private sector is nearly double, primarily due to pensions which government workers receive that the private sector just cannot afford. The number of high-paying jobs has skyrocketed tenfold in the Department of Defense as well as the Department of Transportation. They all vote, and not surprisingly, they never vote for cuts in spending.

The growth of government has occurred on both parties' watches! Nicholas Eberstadt of the *Wall Street Journal* keenly pointed out that the growth has been 5% overall, and higher in Republican presidencies than Democratic ones. This again proves there is not much truth coming out of Washington these days. Their behavior is appalling.

The greatness of America—clearly pronounced in our Constitution and recognized in the U.S. and abroad—has always been reflected in our perseverance, our ability to get things done through hard work, and our fierce drive for independence. With the ascent of big government and the associated high taxes to fund it, the incentives of hard work and entrepreneurism among individuals fade.

And now you know how Team USA got into this difficult predicament. The trend is bigger government. In the next chapter, let's look a bit further at the state of some of the entitlements.

CHAPTER 14
ADDRESSING ENTITLEMENTS

You can't build character and courage by taking away people's initiative and independence. You can't help people permanently by doing for them what they could, and should, do for themselves.

~ Abraham Lincoln
16th U.S. President (1861-1865)

One of the consequences of such notions as 'entitlements' is that people who have contributed nothing to society feel that society owes them something, apparently just for being nice enough to grace us with their presence.

~ Thomas Sowell
Libertarian Economist & Author

The growth of entitlements can best be explained by a few graphs and charts addressing the trends in dollars that are transfer payments, percentages of households receiving benefits (just where the money is going), and percentages of government spending going to entitlements.

First, the trend in entitlements in current dollars paid to individuals is noteworthy.

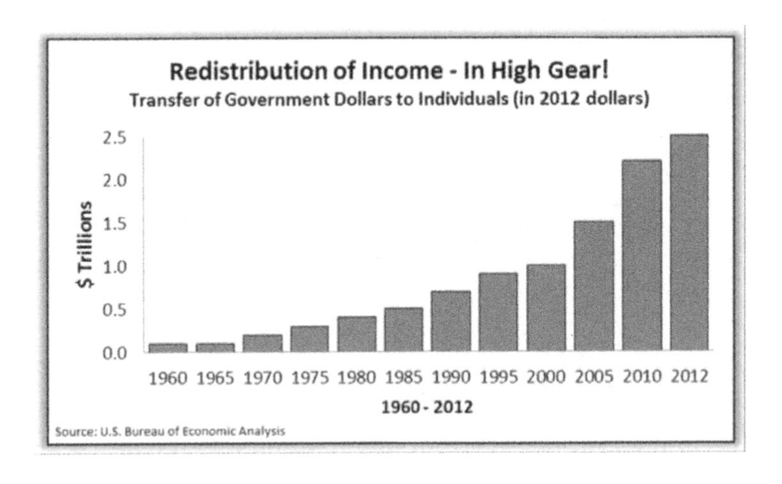

Government payments to individuals in the 1960s barely moved the needle. Social Security had been around for 25 years but collectors lived very few years. Medicare and Medicaid commenced with Lyndon B. Johnson and the payments ascended until 1990. But look at the difference from 2005 and 2012! Herein lays the monumental problem. Now, we are spending over $900 billion per year, or 40% of every government dollar spent, on these two healthcare programs.

Next, and alarmingly so, is the percentage of households receiving benefits from the government.

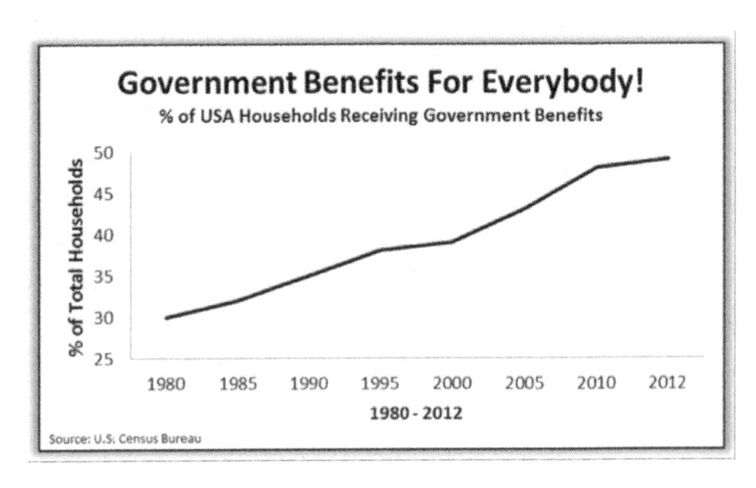

In 1980, approximately 30% of Americans received some type of government aid. We are now touching the 50% line, with the ascent of the last thirty years straight up!

The entitlement figures used by the U.S. Census Bureau are dominated by benefits associated with old age (Social Security and Medicare) and poverty (Medicaid and income maintenance). In order of costs in 2010:

ENTITLEMENT	$ Billion	%
Social Security	$690	
Medicare	518	
"Old Age" (combined)	$1,208	54%
Medicaid	405	
Income Maintenance	265	
Poverty (combined)	$670	30%
Unemployment	140	7%
Other	203	9%
TOTAL	$2,221	100%

So, entitlements are exploding, with the majority going to older people and poor people.

By 2010, entitlement payments accounted for nearly two-thirds of all federal spending, double the percentage it was prior to the 1970s.

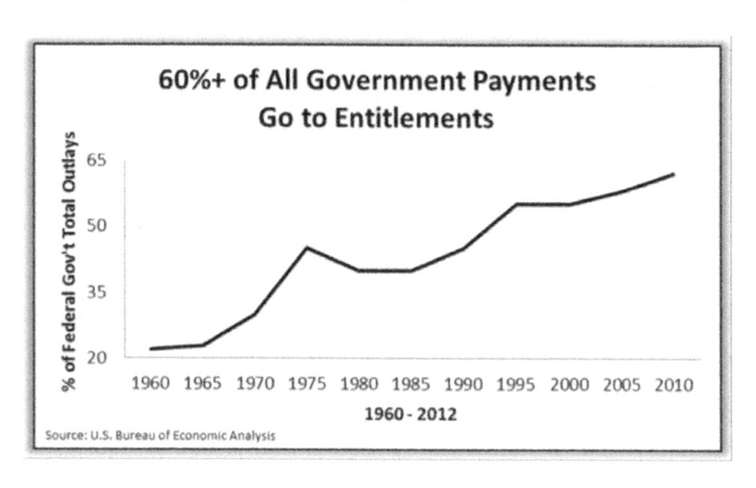

The role of government has flipped over the last forty years from that of a protector with an emphasis on independence and opportunity to one of a redistributionist provider. Note that entitlement payments were just 20% of every dollar spent in 1960. Now it is over 60%!

When addressing entitlements, one should not overlook public policies and their effects on incentives to work. Higher labor participation rates equate to higher GDP, more tax revenue, and fewer government handouts. Food stamps recipients have soared since 2000 and do not correlate with subsequent drops in unemployment associated with the economic recovery. The Supplemental Nutrition Assistance Program (SNAP) has soared 70% since 2008, as asset and income tests have been eased. In fact, the program has grown immensely since 2010 and now there are incredibly almost 50 million recipients! The cost is nearly $75 billion (yes, that's a "b") per year, and looking like it will add itself to the permanent list of entitlement programs. That's 15% of the current U.S. population—nearly three times the number of people on food stamps than in 2000. The eligibility rules have been so broadened that a family of four making over $40,000 qualifies for food stamps. Are you serious? Something is alarmingly wrong here!

The extension of unemployment benefits to 99 weeks was used for years during the Great Recession. It is amazing how many people miraculously find work around week 95, when they are no longer paid to stay at home. It's human nature! But the effect of the presence of these entitlements on the character of American society is alarming.

We see advertisements on TV, billboards along roads and in subways, and webpage banners online offering entitlements of all sorts. Who is paying for all this? You, me, and our unborn children and grandchildren are paying for it.

Disability claims should decrease over longer periods of time, as we are healthier and employ more people in service jobs. In 1990, three million people were disabled. Now we are approaching nine million, or three times as many. This program also must be significantly altered.

So with our existing programs in place (some now describe it as government taking care of everyone "cradle-to-grave"), how will our key economic variables look in the future? Let's assume we attempt to extrapolate current policies.

Gene Epstein of *Barron's* weekly newspaper authored an excellent report in February 2013 entitled "Next Stop, Greece." Much of the next few pages borrow from his observations.

The simplest answer is that our key economic variables will look awful. Continued projected annual deficits, as previously illustrated, roll up into a total debt picture that the Simpson-Bowles Commission summarized as an "unsustainable fiscal path." Why? You guessed it—demographics and entitlements. Despite many economists' pleas that growing our way out is the only way, the answer is still demographics and entitlements.

Let's look at the debt projections as well as the aging population.

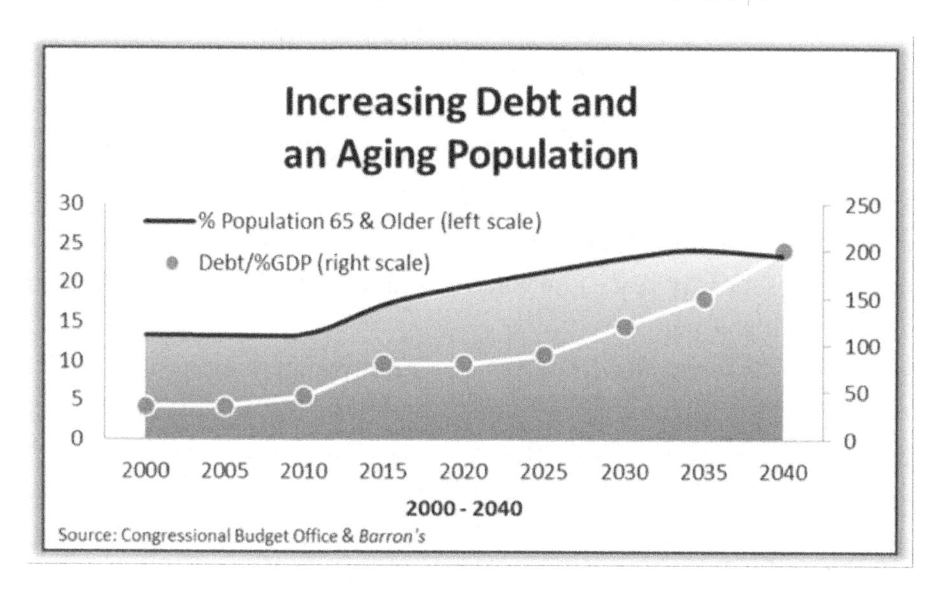

The graph highlights the correlation of two variables—our national debt as percent of GDP and our aging population. The black line represents our debt as percent of GDP, and uses the scale on the right. Historically, debt was around 35%, and then the 2008 to 2012 period increased it to 70%. Yes, over 200 years to get to 35%, and only the last four to double it. Using CBO estimates, the debt is predicted to level off slightly—the calm before the storm. Then in 2023, just a short ten years away, Armageddon commences. Debt as percent of GDP would more than double to a Japanesque 200% level over the next 20-year period, blowing by Greece's current situation in about 15 years.

The red line and the shaded area use the left scale, and vividly illustrate the graying of America. The percentage of Americans 65 years of age or older has been approximately 13% since 2000. The trend has just begun its ascent, and a steep one it is! The number of older people is projected to increase to over 20% in 2030. Demographics are driving entitlements, which are driving huge deficits and raising debt levels. Call it a baby-boom time bomb.

Epstein was brilliant on addressing tax increases on the rich. He pointed out that raising the top rate to 50% on the top 1% of earned income taxpayers (who pay 40% of all the government's take) does virtually nothing to the debt line. Even if you ignorantly assume higher tax rates don't cause rich people to lower their taxable income by changing their behavior and investments, the line would only move by a year or two. Like the smoker who inhales for fifty years—he will die from it eventually. Yes, it is indeed an unsustainable path!

After this Great Recession, we are unfortunately living in a world where capitalism again has been questioned. We continually hear about the working minority "paying their fair share" and "it's all about balance" and "the well-off should be ashamed." The new Pope's inaugural Easter message mentioned the "world still divided by greed looking for easy gain." France elected a socialist to head its country and, not surprisingly, his attempt of raising the marginal tax rate to 75% has been successful, although the Constitutional Council greatly limited the scope and range of the measure. He was then shocked when several of the most wealthy people announced their plans to leave the country. (By the way, I'll bet you anything tax revenue will mysteriously go *down* over time).

We need to educate America again that capitalism is NOT bad or wrong! It is far superior to any other form of government, including socialism and communism. Engendered into that education process should be the notion that successful people operating businesses are not necessarily corrupt on crony capitalism!

There are times when I am completely astonished that a majority of Americans now look at business as the enemy. For generations, people looked up to successful religious leaders, architects, tech entrepreneurs, athletes and rock stars, particularly if they were hard-working Americans. Many wondered, "What makes him tick?" and most were respectful of their life choices, which normally included many personal sacrifices. Oh, and by the way, these people have created jobs for other people who wanted to work.

To improve GDP growth rates, we need to reinstate incentives and enjoy the fruits of our labor! The economy grows faster with incentives, and when it does, more opportunities for advancement are available for those who elect to pursue them. Conversely, as entitlements grow, there seems to be less and less respect for the creators, workers, and entrepreneurs. We are too busy arranging the deck chairs so everyone is in first class—while the boat is sinking. The Titanic must change course.

CHAPTER 15
TODAY'S FISCAL SCORECARD

He that goes a borrowing goes a sorrowing.

~ Benjamin Franklin

I have been a part of numerous conversations throughout the years regarding which economic variables really are important and how they are performing. These variables determine our overall quality of life. They have remained virtually the same for decades—GDP growth, inflation, unemployment, and debt.

Today's fiscal scorecard, below, summarizes the most important variables, where we've been recently, and how we should grade our elected leaders.

VARIABLE	DESIRED RATES	RECENT RATES	GRADE	COMMENTS
1. Real GDP Growth	3-4%	1-2%	C	Best Life Indicator
2. Price Stability (Inflation)	1-3%	1-2%	B+	Avoiding Deflation
3. Unemployment	5%	7%	C	Uncertainty
4. Deficits/Debt % GDP	2-3% / 35%	4-10% / 70%	F	Treacherous
TOTAL GRADE			D+	

Without striving to maintain these variables at healthy levels (within normal ranges), all other variables affecting our daily lives eventually won't matter!

The Economist (magazine) published a special poll in the autumn of 2012. All participants were given a host of issues to opine upon, and asked which of the issues were among their top three concerns. To no one's surprise, the top concern was the economy, with 73% of those polled ranking it high. The health of the economy is a product of the first three variables in my chart above: GDP, inflation, and unemployment. The second most important variable was the budget (ranked high by 41% of the people polled), illustrating that people care about debt and suggesting that our current national debt is looming in the forefront of their minds. The debt/deficit issue is the fourth variable in the chart above, not necessarily fourth in importance, but included in the group of items that Americans focus on the most.

The second tier of important issues from *The Economist* included health care (35%) and education (20%). A list of issues comprised the third and final tier including defense (15%), immigration (14%), the environment (12%), foreign policy (12%), abortion (5%) and crime (3%).

Many other measures should be mentioned regarding today's fiscal scorecard. For example, the median household income has declined, so the typical person is not doing as well as he or she was four or five years ago. Also, deficits per person are an unimaginable $53,000! That's higher by $10,000 than Greece, Italy, Spain, Portugal, and France.

Why am I so concerned about today's scorecard? Because America is focused on everything but the important items—and I fear our leaders in Washington aren't really aware of that! We hear more about gun control, immigration, gay marriage, and abortion than creating jobs, watching our debt, or incentivizing people to invest and grow GDP. If it sounds like I want to scream, I do! And, I am!

For our country to get out of the economic malaise we are experiencing, job creators, risk-takers, and money-makers must not feel demonized. The CBO estimates GDP growth "for next year" to be 3-4%, as predicted so incorrectly for several years now. The constant chatter has been that the more fortunate (maybe the harder working and/or more intelligent worker) should pay more for the privilege of being an American. That just does not sit well with motivated individuals of all shapes, sizes, colors, and political persuasions, particularly when half our country pays zero federal income tax, and the percentage of taxes paid continues to shift responsibility to the higher income end.

We simply cannot continue to think like Keynesians. Big deficits must be paid for, and business people won't invest if the tax rate trajectory continues to climb. Lower your handicaps. Have another cold one. I get to keep 30% of my earnings after all taxes?

The cost of government workers in the jobs bill proposal was absurdly high, and paid with debt that will far outweigh the temporary government-created jobs. Furthermore, government spending has not nor will not trump tax reductions regarding an impact on GDP.

Our huge deficits are a function of stimulus spending, and to a lesser extent less revenue due to the recession. Pundits of the important variables above often distract Americans with other causes of the deficit. They claim the deficit is solely caused by the tax cuts, or the two wars, or even Medicare D. If the deficit was caused by these variables, how could the deficit have been only $161 billion and less than 2% of GDP in 2007, when all these were already in place? Our spending is significantly above our long-term averages of approximately 21% by a wide margin, while revenues are still a bit below their 18% long-term average.

Our overall scorecard rating is *not* good. Yet in spite of this, our ill-fated allegiance to Keynesian spending policies and unsustainable projected debt levels continue to produce sky-high levels of uncertainty.

CHAPTER 16
HEADWINDS: DEMOGRAPHICS, DEBT, DEFICITS, AND MORE

You cannot give up until you have lived out the full extent of your potential, because you have no right to rob me and the next generation of the wealth, treasure, and tremendous gifts buried deep within you.

~ All Souls Day Saying

As all pilots will profoundly say, headwinds can make your flight seem really long.

When you fly into the wind, it slows your speed significantly. Things just take longer and you have to work even harder.

I've spent the bulk of my career in the institutional money management industry. On this path, one saying has proven true repeatedly to me and I believe it will forever withstand the test of time: "Good performance covers the clouds of everything else, and your mistakes and headwinds are then minuscule."

Team USA has some formidable headwinds, and they must be acknowledged in the formation of solutions to our problems. A take-off should sound something like: "Solid GDP growth will overcome all of your headwinds and concerns, and the surpluses will return soon thereafter."

Okay. So what are our headwinds? Unfortunately, we have many.

DEMOGRAPHICS

The first headwind we should discuss further is demographics. The projected aging of America is not at all kind to the income statement or the balance sheet. The double whammy of more people over the age of 65 becoming receivers and slower growth in the workforce will significantly slow GDP and tax revenues. Most estimates, besides the CBO's, say the U.S. long-term growth rate needs to be lowered by ½-1%—for demographics alone.

DEFICIT SPENDING

The current deficit spending, in short, creates artificial GDP growth. It is unsustainable and must be stopped, despite the political rhetoric.

As part of raising the debt ceiling several years ago, our leaders agreed to automatic cuts across the board in early 2013—called a sequester—before raising the debt ceiling again. Well, it materialized, and runaway deficit spending had to be curtailed.

There was much rhetoric about the economic hardships that would supposedly occur in early 2013 from the sequester. Some said much ill-will shall occur, including the safety of our airports. The parks would partially close and GDP would plummet. Here in Kentucky, our local supra (that's *super-super* to me) liberal congressman John Yarmuth (D) opined in our local liberal newspaper how wrong it was that a poor Ft. Knox family was getting a 20% pay cut as part of the sequester. My response in an unpublished letter to the editor was that I too felt sorry for them. But if Yarmuth and his colleagues on both sides of the fence did their job, that would not happen. By the way, I did add a few lines about their focus on immigration, gun control, and gay marriage, noting their complete avoidance of all things financial. Ya think that was the reason it wasn't published?

We need to cut spending as part of a grand bargain. And life as we know it—particularly the entitlements—will change. The sooner, the better.

THE AFFORDABLE CARE ACT

Commonly known as Obamacare, this headwind could be a huge speed bump to economic growth. Some estimates of the total cost are now 40% higher than they were in 2011. Buckle up! Now that implementation recently was botched and parts of it postponed—is reality settling in?

The CBO has estimated the cost and revenue of the Affordable Care Act (ACA).

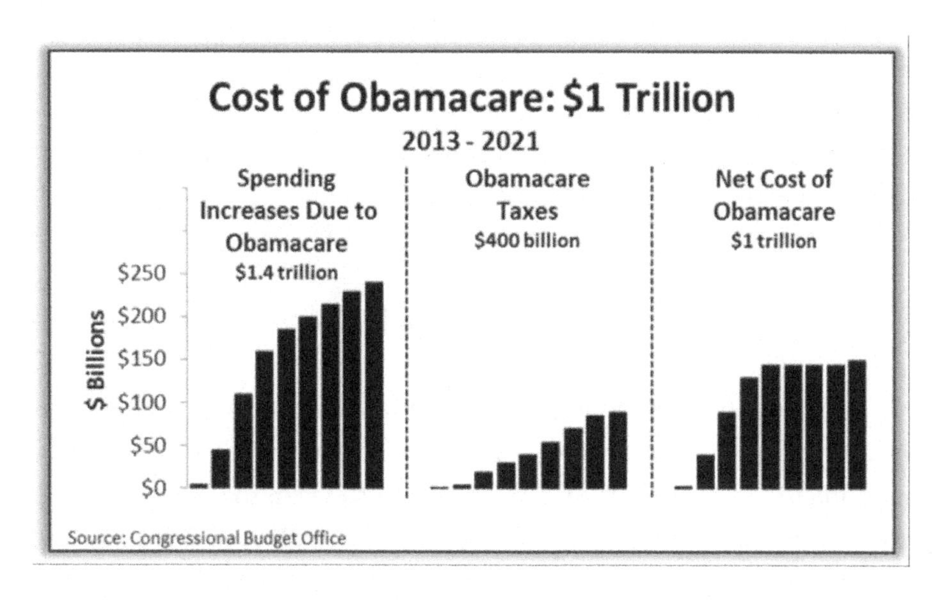

As the graph clearly illustrates, spending associated with the latest and greatest government program far exceeds the anticipated tax revenue. Over a nine-year period (2013-2021), cost will exceed taxes by $1 trillion. The far right graph shows an annual deficit of approximately $150 billion.

Estimates by the CBO of the costs of various programs throughout the years have significantly missed their marks by wide margins. I am fearful the net costs will be much higher. Perhaps very much higher.

2015 will bring a host of realities associated with the ACA. Medicine is becoming a less and less attractive career option, and many doctors will retire rather than working harder for less remuneration. Millions of Americans will unhappily have to choose new physicians in the coming year or two, while paying higher premiums and much higher deductibles and co-pays. It's just simple supply and demand concepts of Economics 101! Longer periods in the waiting room and increased complexities of claims and payments will also occur.

Just stop for a moment and put on your business hat. Under the stipulations of this law, you have to offer healthcare coverage if your business has 50 workers or more. So, you stop expanding as you get close to that number. You offer everyone only 30 hours per week, or you have to provide insurance. There is no conceivable way to think this doesn't slow job creation and decrease job quality!

DEBT SERVICE

Servicing the debt reduces GDP growth in a formidable fashion, particularly when interest rates return to more normal pre-Crisis levels. Even with interest rates artificially low, thanks to the Fed, the debt growth in absolute dollars has grown from $7 trillion to $17 trillion plus. Interest cost estimates for as early as 2016 show we may very well be using 15% of the federal budget to cover interest costs.

So demographics, our essential withdrawal from deficit spending, the unknown effects of Obamacare, and the growing cost of servicing the debt combine to, almost certainly, cause slow GDP growth. Headwinds indeed.

The term "new normal" was first made popular by Mohamed El-Erian, the Chief Investment Officer of Pimco, a leading investment management firm. He suggests a slow, 1% growth rate will be the norm. Many other strategists and economists concur, predicting the 1-2% area is a homerun in light of today's challenges. But recall that the CBO annually says that "next year is our year" and stubbornly returns to their pipedream of old normalcy and a 3-5% growth rate. Smoke another doobie. Incidentally, the Fed estimates have been pretty consistent—with rose-colored glasses. The predictions for "next year" are typically 2% higher than what materializes. And now their divine faith in monetarism (the Fed flooding the market with dollars) is in question.

This is very important because tax revenue is tied to these assumptions. We need revenue to cover our expenses. But what we really need is a strong dose of realism. Our president's 2013 budget projections include the imponderable notion that tax revenue will grow 50% by 2016. How? It is fuzzy math at best, has zero percent chance of happening, and the numbers are fabricated only to justify the continuing spending spree.

We have experienced a recession in every decade, and we are now betting we won't have one. The CBO's spin has us braced for a high growth rate—the likes of which hasn't been seen for a long time and which miraculously won't be interrupted by a slowdown.

Government spending per household has now surpassed the median family income of approximately $50,000. It was approximately 70% of that in 2000. So we've been adding 2-3% more spending per year per family, relative to income... Now that illustrates a growing government!

THE DEBT BALLOON

We discussed the leveraging of America in Chapter 9. Recall that the duration and magnitude of the leveraging process lasted over 25 years—commencing in the early 1980s—and the amount of debt as a percent of after-tax income approximately doubled. There, we used household debt as a percentage of after-tax income.

Another confirmation of the leveraging of the USA is to view household debt as a percent of GDP.

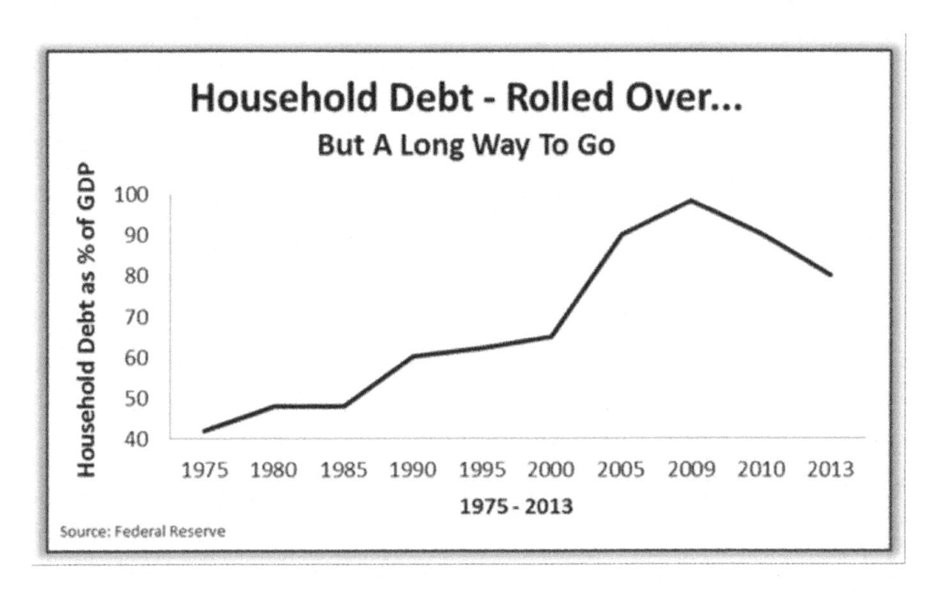

The line was pretty flat from 1975 to the early/mid 1980s when its long climb started. It was typically 50%, on its way to nearly 100%, again over approximately 25 years. And note how it rolled over in 2009. So we are four or five years into a period where households have shunned leverage, but are still way above the longer-term trends.

Some economists profess that we are at the end of the deleveraging process. I say hogwash! The data shows we are probably halfway through! What took 25 years to go up has fallen just halfway down in 4 to 5 years.

Why is this important? It is because consumers—you and me buying things—are 70% of GDP. As a group, we still look pretty levered to me! This is THE major input item in determining GDP growth rates. We simply can't grow at the irrationally assumed 3.5% growth rate with this formidable headwind.

And by golly, these Neo-Keynesians think they are so godly that they can press on the government spending gas pedal and make up for all of it. And that simply has never, nor will ever work. Instead it will only make things worse, as deficits grow and tax rates increase—all while investors are incented to play more golf.

The moral of the story is that we must adjust based on these trends. We cannot attempt to tame the big bear because we just can't do it! Slower growth is a fact, and the deleveraging consumer is playing a key role. Soothsayers of all ilk must be realistic and set lower growth assumptions, which equals lower revenue. Mr. Policymaker, on behalf of my children and grandchildren, please adjust your spending and quit inflating the debt balloon.

GENERATIONAL THEFT

Ignoring the inflation of the debt balloon is downright criminal. And soon, the younger generation will educate themselves (forward them this book?) that they are the ones being slighted.

I know the Neo-Keynesians will argue that their spending is based upon good intentions because the masses are suffering. To those, I offer a free, first-class one-way ticket to the socialistic country of their choice. But strip it all down, throw out far rights and lefts, and take a look at what has worked and what has not. What you end up with is grand larceny—an unpardonable theft from future generations!

Businessmen, hedge fund managers, former Fed members, and economists from all sides concur that government spending levels are unsustainable. There are a few pundits—who are either so politically driven, close to their final judgment day, or simply inclined to repudiate reality—who do not agree. And they just look silly.

Yet still the vast majority of problems lie with Social Security, Medicare, and Medicaid. It is simple math. Those that oppose reform either deny it (though they know it!), think the resiliency of the U.S. economy will eventually take care of it all (impossible), or have a redistributionist agenda, propelled by their jealous disdain for the successful and/or their focus on the less fortunate.

Ultimately, I blame the politicians, as the entire system is in shambles. Most are immoral at best (I really do wonder if they know just how irresponsible they are), playing partisan games, doing whatever it takes to remain in office by catering to their special interests and campaign donors, rather than showing any concern for you and me (who pay the bills).

And the irony of the theft is that the ones who are hurt the most are the lower classes. In the climate of a busted economy, the odds of breaking through the glass ceiling with education, followed by a middle class job, diminishes painfully.

FISCAL STIMULUS vs. TAX CUTS

A headwind that I must mention is the ineffectiveness of backward-looking accommodative fiscal policy. There have been many studies over the last several decades that search for empirical evidence that might determine which spurs economic growth better: a government-spending stimulus or a reduction in taxes propelling the private sector.

The vast majority of these studies agree that changes in fiscal policy focusing on spending and higher taxes are recessionary. Conversely, changes focusing on spending cuts often lead to expansions. This has been true for many developed countries for nearly half a century.

Common sense explains why I have not started (nor do I plan to start) any businesses in recent years. Most investors are willing to risk their capital if they expect that spending and taxes will remain limited and predictable over a formidable period. I have witnessed, and continue to witness, spending increases and tax increases. They do exactly the opposite of what they intend to do regarding economic activity. A strong headwind!

MIDDLE CLASS MYTH

We often hear much about the fall of the middle class and how the bulk of the economic gains of the last 25 years have gone to the top 10% to 20%. I just don't buy it, and I'll tell you why.

Per the Bureau of Labor Statistics, the average hourly wage, adjusted for inflation, has stayed the same for approximately fifty years! Meanwhile, the benefits workers receive have increased substantially (items such as healthcare insurance premiums, vacations, etc.). As an example of benefits typically paid, my family health plan now costs $20,000 a year, of which the company pays $14,000 and I pay just $6,000—and my part is paid with pre-tax dollars. Quite a benefit for the typical worker. Life expectancy for virtually everyone is about ten years longer than it was when I was born!

This all means that the essential elements of having a nice life—having a "roof over your head" and a refrigerator full of food—now cost substantially less as a percentage of take home pay. I had no air conditioning in the car or at home and a manual transmission until I was 25 years old. Nobody but Maxwell Smart and the president had a cellular phone, and Mom did not have a microwave. Vacations were spent at home or within driving distance... We may have gone to the movies (no VCR or cable) or the disco.

My point is that all these items are now considered essential in everyday life. The products that the middle class uses are the same ones used by Bill Gates and the bluebloods! By the way, cars in the mid-1970s were awful—loaded with first generation pollution control catalytic converters. Hilarious in hindsight!

The middle class is doing great… except they now have been trained not to save!

Despite the above, are we—America—doing fine? There is only one way to answer that question, and that is with another question: "Are the dreams and hopes of future generations achievable?" To that I must loudly quip, "Nope. There is no way they're achievable with the debt that you are inheriting!"

INEQUALITY vs. GROWTH

There is an unprecedented level of focus on inequality, particularly relative to the lack of focus on the beauty of economic growth.

Few apolitical economists dispute that economic growth benefits the middle and lower classes. During periods of slow growth like we've experienced since the Great Recession, opportunities for the poor virtually vanish. Witness the meteoric ascent of the SNAP (food stamps) program, unemployment benefits and more.

Economic growth should be the "defining challenge of our time."

The most common measurement of inequality of incomes is the Gini ratio. Developed in 1912 – in a period where entitlements and transfer payments were virtually nil – the Gini ratio ignores entitlements which are over 50% of all government expenditures. When the ratio is corrected for entitlements as well as our progressive tax rates (that indeed redistribute), inequality has declined over the past few decades! And most of the past 25 years focused on capitalism, incentives, and growth!

IMMIGRATION REFORM

Immigration reform and amnesty plans are other examples of our leaders telling half-truths, as most of the costs are hidden from estimates and voters. The facts are simple but they go unrevealed. For example, the typical undocumented immigrant in the USA has just a tenth-grade education. Statistics show households without a high school education receive approximately $4 from Uncle Sam for every dollar they pay in. The CBO claims the cost of reform is just a shadow of the true costs as calculated by the Heritage Foundation.

I must opine that I am for immigration reform, as we need immigration to support the entire system. Progress of societies for centuries has been a function of either population growth or productivity growth, and immigration reform should help immensely regarding population growth and the "browning of America." But we have to do it right!

Specifically, the amnesty proposal specifies that immigrants can't get Obamacare and some other benefits for 13 years. Of course, the CBO's cost projections only go out ten years! By far, the largest costs of amnesty are more than a decade from now when immigrants become eligible for Social Security and Medicare—trillions of dollars on top of these already upside-down programs. The entire program should be focused on attracting (yes, incentivizing) educated immigrants—the way Canada and Australia have done it. Yes, it is a good thing to invite these types of people who are achievers versus receivers. Wake up, Americans!

GLOBAL WARMING

There are dozens of books written about the existence and effects of global warming. They quantify the magnitude of global temperature changes as well as theories on the causes. Some of these books are excellent, and some are written by "save-the-earth" authors.

There are pundits that illustrate that there have been multi-century periods when global temperatures have changed significantly. Examples include the warm Medieval Optimum (700-1200 A.D.) and the cool Little Ice Age (1560-1850 A.D.).

Whatever one believes is a choice. I believe some global warming has occurred. I am in favor of reducing carbon emissions globally. But please educate yourself before pontificating too loudly on this topic.

The United States and other nations signed the Kyoto Protocol in 1997, a treaty for each country to limit carbon emissions back to 1990 levels. The Senate unanimously rejected it in 1999, as developing countries including India and China were exempt. China emits more carbon than the U.S., and collectively with India, is currently opening up 50 new plants per year. We have been unsuccessfully negotiating with them for twenty years.

Since 1997, global temperatures have remained flat. But global emissions have gone up, while U.S. emissions have gone down significantly to 1992 levels. The U.S. is now attempting to regulate the coal industry and prevent any new coal plants, thereby exterminating tens of thousands of jobs. And it will have no effect on climate change, because over 90% of energy use on this planet is outside our control.

What are the chances of a global pact to control emissions? The answer is virtually zero. Why not? China, India, and other developing countries are seeing material increases in the quality of their citizens' lives. Their GDP growth numbers are very healthy! They like the good life, so why should they stop increasing their carbon emissions?

It just all seems silly to inflict a large amount of economic harm on ourselves in the United States, accompanied with an immaterial effect on global warming. We have developed yet another unnecessary, man-made headwind.

It is important to note that I am all-in for addressing climate change in a responsible manner. Leading by example is important! But the U.S. must address these issues with a common-sense approach which includes projecting the magnitude of the impact—both good and bad—from any policies.

PROGRESSIVISM

Many of the trends discussed in this book can be considered part of Progressivism, defined as a political philosophy that advocates gradual social, political, and economic reform through government action. Many are opposed to such so-called "progress," simply because it is not natural and obstructs the "invisible hands" of free markets. Those who dislike progressivism use the "Rule of Law" as their defense, defined as the authority of the law in society.

The central matter is whether the "Rule of Law" has become dominantly positive (government saying what we must do) versus negative (government saying what we must not do). Our forefathers believed the purpose of government was to protect Americans (as in safety), allowing citizens to enjoy life, liberty, and the pursuit of happiness. Period. And no more!

The above trends—most over a quarter-century old—strongly suggest that government now believes differently, and that it can act in a positive fashion. Government officials believe that they can do a better job than the citizens who pay the funds into government, and perform better than the economy would when guided by the "invisible hands." They believe life is better for more people with more government.

In reality, we all know that the only way government can create an economic benefit for some Americans is to first take something away from other Americans. Anyone who tells you differently is not correct.

STUDENT DEBT CRISIS

The ascent of the amount of student debt in the last six years is alarming.

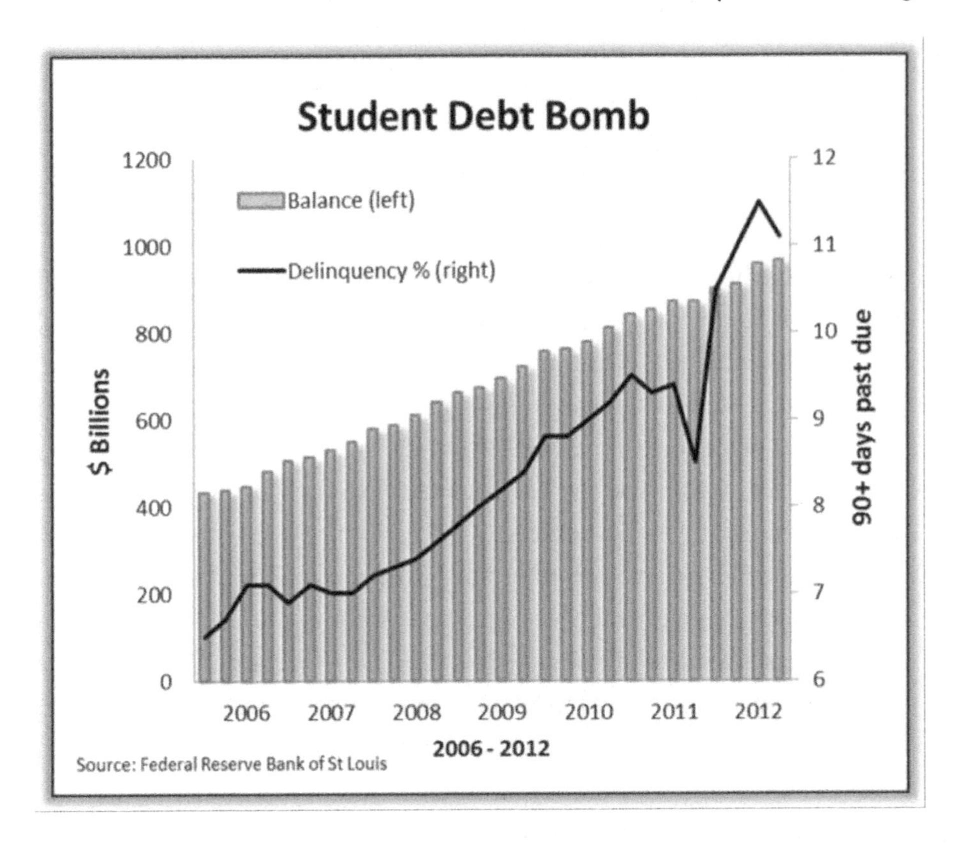

Note that the $400 billion in 2006 has increased to just under $1 trillion in six years! The escalating delinquency rate has increased from 6% to over 11% in the same period. Our government owns over 90% of these loans.

Remember the growth of government assistance in the housing market? The rapid ascent of the number of loans owned by the government—a six-fold increase in just seven years as presented in the graph in Chapter 2—looks eerily familiar.

How can this be? Frankly, there are just too many adults going to college! It is not unlike the Houses for Everyone syndrome in the housing crisis. The government is encouraging kids to go to school who are unqualified just as it encouraged people who were unqualified to buy a new house.

The cost of college has outpaced inflation by nearly 2% for private institutions and nearly 4% for public institutions since 2001. We need to encourage Americans to go to college for a purpose, and it should be evaluated as an investment. That can only be done if the private sector resumes underwriting student debt. Slowing the flow of easy money would unquestionably curtail college costs, assist in cutting the bloated bureaucracies, and result in total costs being better aligned with the rest of our economy.

College costs have skyrocketed just like housing prices did albeit at a more tepid pace—both a function of interfering with the "invisible hands" of capitalism. And yes, that bubble will burst! The process has already begun, as witnessed by the stubbornly high unemployment rate, the declining labor participation rate, and the large number of underemployed. Sadly, they all have huge debts also.

A recent college tour by our president presented proposed solutions to these problems, and I bet you guessed the solution—more government. We are focusing on making one's debt more easily discharged. Already we have some rather silly laws that allow debt to be discharged if you work for the government—as if it is nobler versus working in the private sector. Remember, it is you and I as taxpayers who pay for the discharge of anyone's federal debt.

Recently, a student who was majoring in business while pursuing a minor in accounting visited my office to discuss changing majors. She informed me that she was in the process of changing to a geology major with a minor in music. I kindly inquired what she was going to do after graduation, to which she replied, "I have no idea." My following question was, "How much debt will you have?" She sheepishly replied, "About $100,000. So I oh-so-kindly inquired, "And how will a geology major with a music minor repay the $100,000?" Complete silence. It was as if this fiscally responsible notion was heretical!

I believe society would benefit collectively if we did not grant people the ability to get a degree garnished with government debt that will paradoxically result in the graduate working as a waiter. The waiter would do better in life without the debt. And our country would do better without the defaults on these debts. Let the free market work!

I hope that I do not sound anti-education, as I am the furthest distance from that. Obtaining a degree is well worth it both from a financial and quality of life perspective. But the four-year degree is simply not for everyone.

AMERICA'S "SHIFT TO THE BENCH"

Much attention remains on the unemployment rate. The Fed's qualitative commitment to retain an accommodative monetary policy until it approaches 6.5% is a widely observed evolvement. The flawed measure has fallen from over 9% to more reasonable levels – still a far cry above the long-term natural rate of 5%.

But the unemployment rate does not capture America's "shift to the bench." When you are on a team, you are either playing on the field or you are riding the pine. The Labor Force Participation rate is a much better indicator regarding the American workforce. It is defined as the number of people who are working or looking for work, and it does not include the number of people who are no longer looking for work.

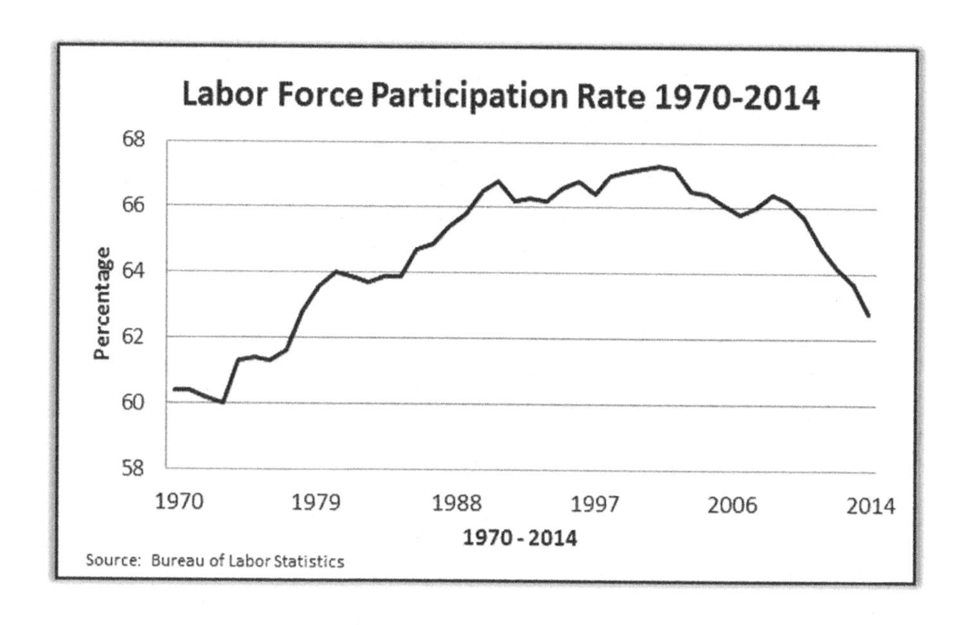

The Labor Participation Rate peaked over ten years ago and has become even less attractive since 2007. Most people would guess that it's a function of the aging baby boomers retiring. However, the rate and trends look the same for the 25-54 age group, suggesting there are more Americans voluntarily shifting to the bench.

There are numerous contributors to this unattractive trend that results in more "receivers" and fewer "achievers." One is the slow GDP growth rate since 2000, a period that includes the Financial Crisis and its anemic recovery. Another is the growth of entitlements—including the large increases of people on disability, food stamps, and welfare. It's just a whole lot easier not to work!

Less people productively paying into the system and more people living off the land—whether content or not—is definitely a headwind for economic progress.

Headwinds abound.

CHAPTER 17
COMMON SENSE POLICIES

My reading of history convinces me that most bad government results from too much government.

~ Thomas Jefferson
3rd U.S. President (1801-1809)

The best two minutes in sports history occurs every year on the first Saturday in May—the Kentucky Derby.

Regarding flashes of brilliance in business and economics, the best two-plus minutes in history, without question, has to be Phil Donahue's 1979 interview with Milton Friedman in which they discussed capitalism.

Donahue: *When you see around the globe, the mal-distribution of wealth, the desperate plight of millions of people in underdeveloped countries; when you see so few haves and many have not's; when you see the greed and concentration of power, aren't you ever, don't you ever have a moment of doubt about capitalism?*

Friedman: *Well first, tell me, is there some society you know that doesn't run on greed? You think Russia doesn't run on greed? You think China doesn't run on greed? What is greed? Of course none of us are greedy—it's always the other fellow who's greedy!*

The world runs on individuals pursuing their self-interest. The great achievements of civilization have not come from government bureaus. Einstein didn't construct his theory under order of a bureaucrat. Henry Ford didn't revolutionize the automobile industry that way.

In the only cases in which the masses escape from the kind of grinding poverty that you are talking about—the only cases in recorded history—are where they have had capitalism and largely free trade. If you want to know where the masses are worst off, it's exactly in the kinds of societies that depart from that.

So the record of history is absolutely crystal clear—that there is no alternative way, so far discovered, of improving the lot of the ordinary people that can hold a candle to the productive activity unleashed to the free enterprise system.

Donahue: *But it seems to reward not virtue but the ability to manipulate the system.*

Freidman: *And what does reward virtue? Do you think a Communist commissar rewards virtue? Do you think a Hitler rewards virtue? Do you think, excuse me, if you'll pardon me, that American presidents reward virtue? Do they choose their appointees on the basis of the virtue of the people appointed or their basis of political clout? Is it really true that political self-interest is nobler somehow than economic self-interest?*

You know I think you are taking a lot of things for granted. And just tell me where in the world you'll find these angels who are going to organize society for us. Well, I don't even trust you to do that!

A classic summary of capitalism and what incentives do—and how it loudly states that it is best for the masses!

As Thomas Jefferson said in the epigram for this chapter, studying history vividly illustrates the perils of too much government. I remain perplexed why some people think it is greedy for one to desire to keep the money that they have earned. It is those same people who think that it is not greedy to take earned money away from the workers!

We just need common-sense policies. We thoroughly know what our Team USA's financials and projections are, as well as how we got here. In addition, I have qualified and quantified the magnitude of the entitlement programs, and addressed the key variables that should be addressed on the fiscal scorecard. With the headwinds upon us, we have some tough choices.

I have divided my thoughts of what should be included in the construction of a common-sense plan and solid economic policies into five areas: Economic Way of Thinking, Taxes, Spending, Social Issues, and Incentives.

Within each of these five areas, I have made recommendations for "Policies to Emphasize" and matters on which we should "Revisit Our Thinking."

ECONOMIC WAY OF THINKING

Policies to Emphasize:

1. Reinstate the American way of embracing capitalism.

2. Admit that demographics control and entitlements are huge.

3. Educate yourself on studies that prove big government equals slower growth.

4. Incorporate realistic assumptions into the CBO budgets.

5. Listen to credible solutions like the Simpson-Bowles Plan.

6. Insist that the Fed present a credible withdrawal strategy to the monetary experiment of our era.

7. Study the Laffer Curve, and its twin Reaganomics, including tax rates, regulations, and size of government. (All are 180 degrees away from the policies of today).

8. Learn from the mistakes of others—namely Keynesian policies disproved in the 1960s and 1970s.

9. Make a commitment to get debt to a manageable 35% of GDP within the decade.

Revisit Our Thinking:

1. Realize that as an American, Americans just do not want socialism.

2. Eliminate Keynesian thinking—even he recanted before death!

3. Stop growth of the size of government.

4. Stop increasing regulation as it thwarts growth.

5. Don't punish the saver, including limiting the dollar amounts in IRA.

6. Discontinue penalizing the successful worker with inheritance taxes; it is a minuscule part of federal revenue and is the ultimate example of redistribution.

7. Stop thinking that government is a good private-equity firm.

8. Stop denying that longer-term unemployment benefits have not driven up the natural unemployment rate, à la Europe.

9. Cease arguing that a major crisis will not develop with large debt levels.

10. Stop publishing very unrealistic studies that show the optimal tax rates are 73% to 83%.

11. Eliminate large agricultural subsidies—let the "invisible hands" work!

TAXES

Policies to Emphasize:

1. Reform the tax code.

2. Create competitive corporate and LLC rates.

3. Study the economic policies of the Depression era, including Hoover and Smoot-Hawley—both demonstrations of the fallacy of taxing America into prosperity.

4. Realize that capital gains rate...

   a. *cuts* indeed increase revenue (like in 1979, 1983, 1997, and 2003), and

   b. *raises* do not (as we saw in 1987 to 1996).

5. Admit that marginal tax rates affect incentives and investment decisions.

6. Study up on zero and low state tax rates—these foster jobs and population growth! For example, witness…

   a. the increases in Florida, Texas, Tennessee, Arizona, and North Carolina, and

   b. the decreases in high tax rate states in New York, Illinois, Ohio, California, and Oregon.

7. Consider a zero capital gains rate—which results in job creation and subsequent tax revenue from more jobs!

Revisit Our Thinking:

1. Learn that tax rate increases will result in less tax revenue.

2. Stop thinking lower capital gains rates are loopholes. Low rates create incentives, thus investments, thus jobs, and thus tax revenue.

3. Cease threatening to eliminate municipal bonds—the cost of capital for states goes up!

SPENDING

Points to Emphasize:

1. Agree to cuts now and over ten years.

2. Acknowledge entitlement reform is paramount.

3. Execute pension reform, reducing the large benefit amounts for relatively few years of service in the public sector.

4. Employ many easy techniques to make Social Security solvent.

5. Consider limiting many Medicare services in the final months of life, as a large percentage of America's healthcare expenses are associated with this problem—unlike all other developed countries!

6. Study Canada's austerity and resulting surpluses.

Revisit Our Thinking:

1. Act as if tax increases will pay for large and growing entitlement programs.

2. Stop spending on and hiding of special interests.

3. Cease focusing on minutia cuts that don't even amount to 1% of the problem.

4. Eliminate the duplication of many federal programs.

5. Stop temporary programs like the CARS (the Car Allowance Rebate System, a.k.a. "cash for clunkers"). Temporary programs do nothing to stimulate demand.

6. Reduce all agencies 10% now in commitment to pay for past and current performance. (With such a performance in the private sector, you'd be fired!)

SOCIAL ISSUES

Points of Emphasis:

1. Reinstate patriotism and responsibility—for our kids!

2. Address the major sources of spending: Social Security, Medicare, and Medicaid.

3. Accept responsibility for one's position, and stop blaming others.

4. Reinstate federal work regulations and Clinton's welfare reform; welfare cases decreased 50% over the eight years following implementation.

5. Make politicians have the same benefits as taxpayers. Amen.

6. Realize right to work states are growing and creating more jobs!

7. Educate yourself on the effect of higher minimum wages; it brings the most harm to the least skilled, as businesspeople adjust and hire fewer workers.

8. Stop regulating everything and capitalizing on a crisis.

9. Allow us to become energy independent.

10. Reduce the size of government through attrition—even the smallest amounts add up.

Revisit Our Thinking:

1. Stop being totally self-absorbed Americans.

2. Cease spending so much time on non-issues, intentionally distracting America from the real ones.

3. Stop beating up the businessman for creating and building his business.

4. End earmarking: it is crony capitalism.

5. Stop allowing Congress to benefit from insider trading. An unfathomable law!

INCENTIVES

Points to Emphasize:

1. Acknowledge that incentives matter!!!

Revisit Our Thinking:

1. Eliminate redistributionist mentality.

2. End extended unemployment and incent people to get back to work!

In summary, common sense policies are needed for America. And they are really common sense! Let's restore our greatness and love of capitalism. We need tax reform, spending cuts, and a restoration to patriotism and responsibility. Without an abrupt change addressing the structural problems now upon us, the USA will find itself in a terrible, economic climate for an extended period of time, as many other great countries have unhappily discovered. My final recommendation echoes that of Thomas Jefferson: Study history!

PART IV. INVESTMENT IMPLICATIONS

We have discussed the causes and consequences of the Great Recession, stressed the importance of sound economic policies, and also delineated that Team USA has a spending problem and significant headwinds. What are some investment implications going forward in light of our current economic state?

In this section we will discuss seven guiding principles of investing—tidbits of wisdom derived from thirty years' experience in the investment management industry. What should one do with their hard-earned assets? We'll discuss some major asset classes that should be a part of your investment strategy, and a few that should not. And then, some final thoughts on the Great American Reset...

CHAPTER 18
SEVEN GUIDING PRINCIPLES

We must lay hold of the fact that economic laws are not made by nature.
They are made by human beings.

~ Franklin D. Roosevelt
32nd U.S. President (1933-1945)

There are a few questions that I have been asked more frequently since the Great Recession. "Should I incorporate the knowledge of our current economic state into my investment process? Will it perversely cause me to obtain less return and/or add more risk? If so, how do I incorporate this knowledge into my investing process?"

There are many books, theories, and lectures on the perils of attempting to predict markets, as well as their correlations to economic growth (or lack thereof). Some say buy-and-hold strategies are best because the typical investor naturally and erroneously buys high when the world seems peachy, and sells low when problems have been identified by John Q. Public. The selling typically occurs just after prices fully reflect the negative news.

I will argue, successfully so, that paying attention to key economic trends can be immensely influential to making successful investment decisions! Timing trends and market entry and exit points are far from easy to identify, and attempting to do so is not advisable for the average investor. But neither I nor you, as a reader of this book, have ever strived to be ordinary, or average at anything. So let's look at my seven favorite guiding principles that pertain to investing before we discuss the next five to ten years.

PRINCIPLE 1: MARKETS LOVE TO PARTY... and PARTY HARD INDEED!

Corollary: Every big party comes to an end, and the aftermath is never pretty.

As we will discuss in Part VI, we have had Tulip Mania and real estate booms and busts. In my lifetime, I've seen bubbles in real estate, technology, stocks, and real estate again. Whether it was portfolio insurance, long-term capital, B2B, or CDOs, in every case, there was the promise that this "new" concept, techno-gadgetry, or novel approach was going to permanently change everything. The Internet and securitization, for two examples, indeed changed things substantially—but not without many side effects.

So the investment implication is to not get lured to sleep at the wheel once we embark into a new era! You should invest with it, but you must realize a correction is about to be born, and that the asset class is heading back to its mean—and then it will get worse! Before the next leg up can materialize, the correction must overshoot on the downside, thereby wiping out all excesses in the cleansing process. A new bull market in that asset class will be born—eventually—and the ascent toward (and beyond) the mean will ensue.

PRINCIPLE 2: SOUND ECONOMIC POLICIES ARE ESSENTIAL FOR LONG-TERM SUSTAINABLE WEALTH CREATION

Corollary: Both the Fed and Washington have to create an economic environment of price stability at the forefront, and realize that incentives matter!

Over longer periods of time, the stock market plays a significant role in wealth creation. It is driven by earnings and the expansion and contraction of the price/earnings (P/E) ratio. Earnings tend to track economic growth closely in normal economic times. P/E movements are driven by the existence of sound economic policies that promote low and stable inflation as well as by investor sentiment, i.e., how confident investors are about the future of the economy and the associated policy trends.

The investment implications from the Great Recession vividly illustrate the importance of sound policies. As summarized in Chapter 2, the lax legislation allowing everyone to purchase a home with low interest rates and lots of leverage spiraled into a period of substantial economic losses.

PRINCIPLE 3: FUNDAMENTALS and VALUATIONS ARE THE FOUNDATION; TECHNICAL ANALYSIS CAN GIVE YOU THE EDGE!

Corollary: Charting all investments provides huge benefits to creating wealth.

Understanding the fundamentals of every investment you might be considering seems like common sense, but the effort often goes neglected. The products, trends, competitors, management, and resulting financial ratios are influential in the success of the investment.

Valuation levels such as P/E ratios, yield, and price-to-book are also important in investing. How a market or individual stock trades relative to other markets should always be part of the investment decision-making process.

But in order to properly buy/sell and increase your ability to create wealth, technical analysis should be employed. It is a security analysis methodology for forecasting prices through the study of past market data, primarily price and volume.

Technical analysis importantly assists you in winning the loser's game in several ways. First, you can normally avoid the torpedo effect—or stocks on a death march. Just one 75% loss on an individual issue—no matter how diversified one's portfolio is—materially influences total return. Second, technical analysis assists investors in finding good entry points, and works well in most bulls and bears. The only exception may be in the initial euphoria of a new long-term bull.

PRINCIPLE 4: COMMON CHARACTERISTICS OF BULLS and BEARS

Corollary: Breadth and sentiment are important for both bulls and bears; long-term ranges are simple facts of investing.

Bull markets are born out of extreme pessimism, brought on by bad policies, a financial crisis, or a valuation correction. Bulls accelerate briskly and consolidate before resuming another leg up, then repeat it again. They last 15 to 20-plus years with average annual gains of over 15%. True bulls are not led by just a few captains, but are broad in nature with virtually all stocks participating.

Bears commence with a hard fall, followed by a partial positive retracement, before taking the long-and-winding road down. Bears have a trading range—annual gains in the low single digits—and last 14 to 18 long years. When the public has increased its allocation to equities to very high levels, the bear is just around the corner. John Q. Public always buys the top of the market. Even more perversely, when the Wall Street strategists have their asset allocation recommendations to stocks at the high end of the range, you better run faster than Usain Bolt! They are the ultimate contrarian indicator.

I've read much about the unparalleled party of the 1920s, and the living-dead hangover of the 1930s. (The 1990s was my one and only comparable period of rollicking good fortune… close anyway, but not quite the 1920s.) My favorite story of the Roaring Twenties was one attributable to a wealthy investor named Mr. Joseph Kennedy. He was the father of our 35th President John F. Kennedy, his illustrious brother

Robert, and longtime Senator Ted. Joe was getting his shoes shined in 1929, and the shoeshine guy was giving him advice on which stocks to buy. If that's not a signal that we are at the top of the market, what would be? Folklore has it that he "sold the farm" and missed the 90% stock market crash. Knowledge of trends and bulls and bears can be quite profitable!

Let's fast-forward to the spring of 2000. This was our generation's 1929! "It's déjà vu all over again!" quoth the great Yogi Berra.

My colleague, mentor, market historian, and partner of many years is a man named Mick Heyman. He and I were in Manhattan that spring to hear the latest Wall Street-speak (and yes, we often used the information as a contrarian indicator). We made two great observations that trip. First, we were the only people in New York City wearing ties, and the casual dress trend was more than just a blip. Second and most importantly, we realized the 1982-2000 big bull was in its ninth inning. Why? When two cab drivers recommend stocks to two money managers of over $17 billion, is that not reminiscent of Joe Kennedy's shoeshine boy? Our guts and experience growled oh-so-loudly that the frothy market was close to its pinnacle. Several months later, we sold our asset management firm, handsomely enhancing our personal balance sheets. (The cab drivers' picks, by the way, included Cisco and Qualcomm—which both cratered more than 75% over the next few years.) The investment implications of knowing history, knowing there are long-term ranges, and watching trends can be very beneficial.

As a recreational pilot of single-engine aircraft, I have learned that paying attention to "which way the wind is blowing" and the speed it is blowing is paramount! It is no different in investing. Trying to enhance wealth without knowledge of the investment environment you are stepping into is definitely a loser's game.

PRINCIPLE 5: SAVOR THE GOOD TIMES

Corollary: Bulls make rock stars, bears make professors.

When times are not good, such as the 1968-1982 sideways bear market, the daily grind is just that. My forever friend William Chandler, a wonderful Yale grad who has an excellent perspective of markets and life, commenced his investment career in 1968 when the Dow was at 1000. Move (very slowly) forward some 14 years to the fall of 1982, and the market was at 782. And inflation in the 1970s was nothing to sneeze at—on occasion, double digits! Thus, Bill experienced a long period of wealth creation in reverse. Both in nominal and real terms, investors were way behind.

This author was fortunate enough to commence his career in the very early innings of the bull market that commenced in 1982. The annual rate of return on stocks was an eye-opening 18%! With the wind at your back, with very solid economic policies (Washington—take note!) AND an understanding of history and the bull, *every day* was a day at the beach. Savor the good times, and thoroughly enjoy your temporary stint as Rock Star.

I must attribute some of my thoughts to Wall Street guru Bob Farrell, whose writings were rather influential to me in my early days, particularly regarding technical analysis, the importance of being lucky, and other excellent tidbits of wisdom.

So, this author is now a professor, but still a money manager. Enjoy the bull, grind through the bear, and brace for the coming storm. Then profess and write a bit, imparting some wisdom learned. Now that's happiness!

PRINCIPLE 6: PROJECTED RETURNS DRIVE WEALTH CREATION

Corollary: Past performance is NOT a predictor of future performance.

Most investment professionals will base their predictions on long-term historic rates of return for the major asset classes. For example, stocks deliver 10-11% per year over longer periods of time and bonds 6-7% per year. And guess what? That's important to know, but that means nothing going forward!

The equity market indeed has delivered 10-11% since the inception of solid return data in the 1920s. But most of the years since have been in a 3% GDP growth rate environment! Realistic GDP growth assumptions going forward as earlier presented are 1-2% per year. This makes 10-11% for equities impossible over the long term.

An even better example is returns from fixed income. Historically they have been 6-7%, but going forward, it is mathematically impossible to even get 4% per year over the next five to ten years. I've invited numerous of my investment professional friends to take the other side of that bet that the total return from bonds will be zero over the next five years: I've found zero takers.

I follow the projected returns for all asset classes from numerous large investment and consulting firms as well as the large endowment funds. They are intellectually superior, fundamentally sound, and extremely important in managing portfolios to achieve the highest return/lowest risk allocations.

PRINCIPLE 7: ALTERNATIVE ASSET CLASSES WORK!

Corollary: The traditional 60% stock / 40% bond allocation will NOT work going forward!

In the 1980s, I became intrigued with the sophisticated, unique investment approaches of the largest endowment funds including Harvard, Yale, and Stanford. They each have pursued a more diversified investment approach, where they typically dedicate a larger allocation to real estate, hedge funds, and private equity versus the typical university or individual investor. Exposure to fixed income is lowered and domestic equities are further diversified with more assets dedicated to foreign stocks.

And the result is? Their portfolios typically deliver an additional 2% per year versus the typical investor asset mix, and importantly with similar or less risk. In addition, investing with alternative asset classes makes the return correlation of the portfolio compared to the market far less (0.4) than the typical asset mix (0.7).

So there really is such a thing as a free lunch? Granted these investment strategies, which I personally utilize and are a huge reason that I sleep so well at night, have periods of underperformance when the stock market roars. But through the entire cycle, the critics are crushed as returns (net of all fees!) are higher and the correlation to the market is far lower.

A vivid memory of mine occurred in 2003 where I was on the wrong end of the growth of the alternative investment strategies. As a long-only equity manager for the prestigious Centre College, we had bettered the S&P benchmark by just over 2% per year during the prior nine years. That was better than over 90% of our peers and certainly nothing to get fired about... except when the committee adopted the large endowment model of having a higher exposure to alternative investments.

Alternatives really do work—particularly if one has access to the better managers and strategies.

CHAPTER 19
THE GREAT AMERICAN RESET

The darkest hour in any man's life is when he sits down to plan how to get money without earning it.

~ Horace Greeley
Founder, Libertarian Republic Party

When pontificating about the future, virtually every strategist, economist, and money manager either starts with long-term historic norms, or extrapolates the past. I have not seen many asset allocation quizzes (intended to determine one's risk profile) that do not recommend 60-70% stocks, 30-40% bonds. And guess what? They are all probably wrong.

For years, we assumed that over longer periods of time stocks beat bonds by 4-5%. If stocks returned 10-11% annually, then bonds should yield 5-7%. But huge assumptions are made in those figures, including the direction of P/E ratios, dividend yields, and interest rate levels and directions. Also important is the appropriate amount of the risk associated with the required incremental return of investors in stocks.

Many and most have been wrong since 2000. There are no guarantees on any prognostications of any kind in any era! But there are some very true correlations over longer periods of time, and they can assist investors in enjoying preferential rates of return in contrast to buying securities and putting them in the drawer for decades.

First, the foundation of finance, in theory and in practice, rests on the presumption that all investments are valued using the present value of the cash flows plus the present value of the terminal value, discounted back at the required rate of return. The internal rate of return, or IRR, is simply a function of the risk free rate (currently use 2%) plus an appropriate risk premium associated with the risk attached to that asset class, which is simply a function of its volatility. This rule will never change when determining what an investment is worth.

The 50% plunge in the stock market at the commencement of the Financial Crisis and the required 100% increase to get back to the same level has now occurred, securing its story in the history books. The peaks and valleys did not constitute a fun ride in any aspect. If you study history, you should not be surprised that the rebound indeed occurred in some very suspect economic times. So now what?

Let's look at the markets for the next five to ten years from a top-down, macro-economic perspective. Influential factors will be the political environment, the economic environment, and inflationary expectations. Let's briefly look at each of those factors and then the major asset classes used by most investors.

POLITICAL ENVIRONMENT

The political climate that relies on emotion is a show-stopper. Period. If you listen solely to your heartstrings, the music will stop. A return to critical thinking from political leadership must materialize. John Mauldin called it the *Endgame*—some bang, pop, slam (not a boom) that will result in what I call the "Great American Reset." This will involve asset valuation changes, currency devaluations, and a fall of capitalism as we know it. Supra ugly!

The reason is that economic fundamentals matter. Deficits will continue if entitlement spending is not restructured and the programs are recognized as structural dinosaurs. The debt will consume us into a multi-decade period of economic hardship and malaise. And it's all because we spend aimlessly.

Our course of action must be altered or America's economic roller-coaster will lurch off its tracks in the next five years, ten maximum. It will trump the easy money policy of the Fed and the long-term trend in equities discussed later in this chapter.

ECONOMIC ENVIRONMENT

We will need to shift our focus to the important economic variables and the scorecard if we are to avoid the Reset. Let's dream for a moment. Assume that we recognize the facts and accept the scandalous acts of both political parties over the last ten years as spilt milk, and we are now embarking on a concerted effort to do damage control and enact preventative steps for the sake of posterity.

In this scenario, we would get the major primary variables moving toward their long-term targets—approximately 3% growth, 5% unemployment, and 2-4% inflation (okay, even if it is a little higher...). Ben Bernanke's "Hail Mary" of super-easy monetary policy worked! He rides into the sunset pumping his fist like Doug Flutie. Victory!

Secondarily, what would some other items of focus look like? Plenty of cheap energy would be available for all. By the way, I do not mean solar, but rather oil, gas, and coal. Additionally, we would make great progress on immigration but we must remedy the programs that make it easier not to work versus becoming an old-fashioned hardworking American.

INFLATIONARY EXPECTATIONS

The major fork in the investment implications road was probably reached in 2013, and it involves inflationary expectations. Before investing in this new era, and prior to altering your portfolio, you have to answer just one question: "Are we entering a period of deflation— à la Japan—or are we going to have mild or higher inflation?"

If you think the voluminous efforts of the Fed will *not* work, and they will not keep us out of deflation, then you invest one way. That scenario says there continues to be a growing debt level, and thus expectations for higher tax rates increase. This destroys the animal spirits, and incentives go back in hibernation. Slow GDP growth, deflation, low tax revenues, and a growing debt. Return *of* capital is OK, as your money buys more. Call this scenario "risk off."

Specifically, when deflation occurs, just keeping your money is a big win, as it will buy more next month than it does now. Preferred asset classes are led by fixed income instruments of most any maturity and class. The income produced—how ever little it may be—is worth more on a real, after-inflation basis. Cash works, even though you are basically getting your money back. The dollar is good. Avoid stocks and any asset class highly correlated to stocks, including junk bonds.

On the other hand, if you believe that Fed policy will finally work, and that the lag time was just longer-than-normal, you invest in a different fashion, focusing on "risk on."

ASSET CLASSES IN AN INFLATIONARY ENVIRONMENT

Buy stocks! The rate of return will keep up with or surpass inflation over the duration. The Fed is pushing you into equities for any return or yield. Odds are high that the total return on intermediate term bonds will be a 0% annual rate of return over the next five-year period, as coupons are minuscule and loss of principal always materializes when economic activity heats up.

And real estate is a very good investment in inflationary times. Be careful in your purchases, and realize private real estate sometimes has a negative yield, due to upkeep and carrying costs. But it is in this "risk on" type of investing environment that real estate makes sense.

What about gold as an investment? Does it perform in periods of inflation and deflation? Yes and yes. The problem with investing in gold is that it could go well in "risk off" environments, where deficits are driving stock prices down and gold is a safe haven. On the other hand, it has been a good hedge against inflation (as all precious metals). Gold has become an asset class for most investors to hedge risk in the last ten years, driven by uncertain economic times and the availability of it in an exchange traded fund (ETF) format. But many are reconsidering such wisdom with questions surrounding the frequently used ETF for gold in the SPDR gold trust (a.k.a. "GLD"). Are there really enough assets to back GLD? It's a legitimate question. In the long run, however, I question gold's luster as an asset class. Pun intended.

Private equity investments remain an attractive asset class albeit much lower returns than in recent decades. High fee rates are associated with private equity, and such fees rule out at least half the managers. Investors are not compensated with the additional return versus the public markets, if any, after considering their fees, illiquidity, and risk levels. However, the better private equity managers are worth investing with… although the returns will not be like they were in the past. Their net IRR should be higher than the public markets, but the illiquidity and longer time frames reduce their attractiveness. Nonetheless, private equity remains a viable asset class for the wealthiest sector, even though these managers are dependent upon the public sector for exit strategies. The typical investor should skip this asset class due to the lack of access to the best managers.

Hedge fund investing typically has been used to get stock market-like returns with a much lower risk profile, as variability of cash flows is low. However, in today's environment, returns have lagged considerably, and their role must be reevaluated. Hedge funds should not be used as a non-correlated asset class, as most have been so classified. They should be used only as a source of income, but one must realize that loss of principal, despite a large level of diversification, can occur.

Finally, the bubble of all bubbles—the bond market—must end in the next five years. Bonds have experienced a 30-plus year bull market, as interest rates began decreasing in 1981.

There is only one way for interest rates to move, and it's up! Sure, there is a possibility that we can have a 1% ten-year bond in the next few years. If we do, times are tough and the Fed never used its exit strategy—because it didn't exit! If so, the lag effect of monetary policy never occurred, and the textbooks will be rewritten again.

The current yield curve is simply unimaginable compared to normal times.

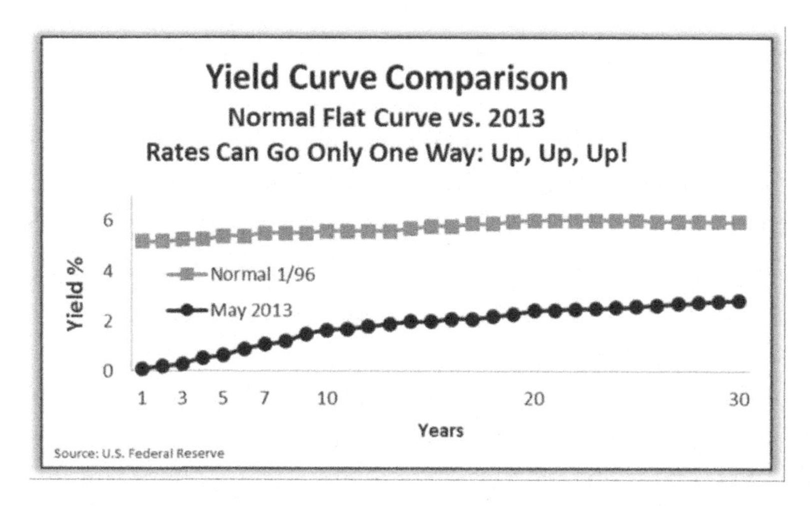

There are two yield curves drawn here. The highest is a typical one, where the longer the maturity, the higher the yield needs to be to compensate for the risk, yet at a diminishing rate. This "normal" yield curve, while it's a bit flatter than the *average* normal, compensates investors for going out on the curve where there is the associated risk of principal. The lower yield curve is one typical of the current era with extremely accommodative monetary policies. It still amazes me that you must look ahead five years to get 1%.

Do you get the picture? Rates are incredibly low *and* far from the state of normalcy established throughout my 30-year career. The interest rate risk is incredibly asymmetric. You need to go less than halfway back to normal (just a few percentage-points increase), and your total return for five years for most all bonds will be negative.

We have successfully played whack-a-mole on the inflation dragon for years, never letting his head dart too far out of the hole. Now we have fought deflation thanks to "Helicopter Ben" (Bernanke flinging money in all directions), and with the amount of medicine being applied, we will have inflation of some sort. Low inflation environments are a panacea for equities, while higher inflation rates cause many problems (take a time machine back to the 1970s to see for yourself). Just remember that, typically, equities keep up with inflation, and bonds do not.

STOCKS FOR THE LONG HAUL... AGAIN!

Professor Jeremy Siegel's 1994 book called *Stocks For The Long Run* became an essential item for any money manager or market historian's bookshelf. In summary, Dr. Siegel proves that decade after decade, the only way to accumulate wealth is through investing in the stock market. The effects of inflation further made his case that the equity market is the only place to invest.

And he was correct... until the 2000 to 2010 decade. Somehow, we had a 30% fall, as the dot-com boom corrected, followed by a 50% correction from the Financial Crisis. And *voila* bonds outperform stocks in the decade, even though bond yields commenced the decade at historically low rates.

But things are quite different now. Yields are lower than low. The Fed used all of its tools and more, and stock valuations are more reasonable.

Most say that the rally back to 2007 highs in stocks illustrates the worst is over economically, and the easy money in stocks has already been made. Or, are we in the early stages of the next great bull market? History provides some suggestions.

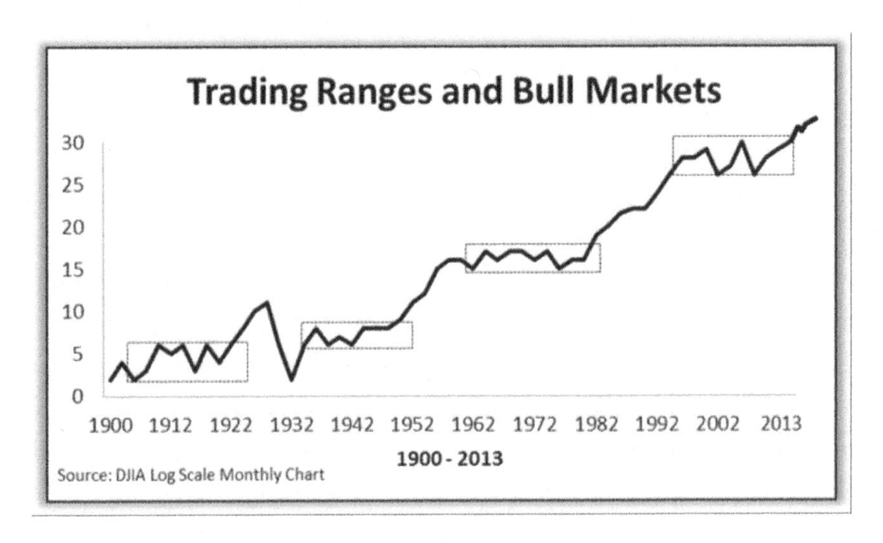

The stock market has returned approximately 10% per year, but you may notice from the above chart, there are eras of immaterial advances called "trading ranges," followed by periods of material advances associated with bull markets. Sideways markets typically last 18 to 19 years, taking their time "making a base," and then head off to the races. And they go for a few decades, with annual rates of return at approximately 15% or more. This is as real as it gets when talking about how means (averages) are formed—they rarely are represented but instead have periods far from the mean on both sides.

William Chandler, fellow historian mentioned earlier, remains an astute investor. A market historian for nearly fifty years, he describes this concept (illustrated in the above chart) as the only thing that really matters in wealth creation. We have been in the multi-year trading range, thereby range-bound (stuck in the boxes), going nowhere for approximately 15 years. It seems we have broken out, and the next new multi-decade bull market has begun, where returns can be almost double the long-term averages.

Note that range-bound periods typically have several "tests" of both the downside and the upside—levels that define the range—and are incredibly resilient.

The 1997 through 2013 range is indeed getting long in the tooth for all of us, around 16 years old. The 666 to 1,565 S&P range was pierced in April 2013, opening the door to a new trending bull market. The next pullback held some key resistance levels *and* the subsequent rally closed above its prior peak, thus the next era has commenced! It is still early in the second inning, with plenty of time to make money. The biggest problem of this prophecy (and any technical analysis prophecy) is that the number of tests of the bottom support levels and upper resistance levels within the range was fewer than the typical range. That presents pause, and suggests that we could possibly have one more down-leg before we really set sail.

Regarding the types of stocks to invest in, there exist long-term secular trends, as well as shorter-term cyclical trends. In long-term trending bull markets, growth stocks are best for the long haul, with cyclical corrections every three to five years. If we are in a range-bound state, old fashioned down-and-dirty value stocks normally outperform.

So *Stocks for the Long Run* has returned? **There is a high probability we are out of the range and have entered the second inning of a new bull market!** The probability we are not is much lower, where we'd test lower levels. Those levels are probably in the middle of the range, thus a retrenchment of approximately 30%.

As we remain in a period of slow GDP growth, the cushion or margin for error is narrower to the zero GDP growth line. Let me assure you with confidence that we will have more frequent recessions due to the narrow gap and slow growth. Associated with that will be more frequent stock market corrections. That's what I mean by "Buckle Up!" The market will be volatile!

Investors should watch P/E multiples and trading ranges. Realize that you are somehow in the early innings of a trending bull market. The fundamentals to why will be clearly explained... in hindsight. Trust the trend and the trend is your friend.

A WORD OF CAUTION WITH EQUITIES

Investing in the equity market can be harrowing, and in the future, changes to the headwinds discussed could make it even more volatile. Stocks give positive returns much more frequently—approximately 70% of the time—than negative returns. Yet intra-year percent changes in your typical year are approximately 15%. There are corrections in all types of markets that occur fairly routinely in most years.

Bull markets begin with a change in the direction of interest rates called "inflection points."

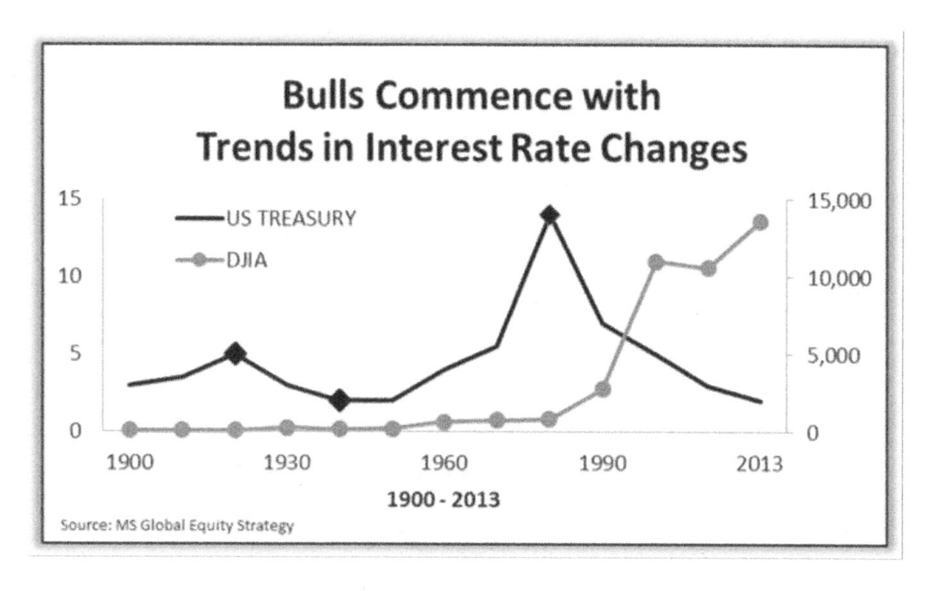

The great bull markets of the 1920s, 1950s, and 1980s/1990s each had a change in the direction of long-term interest rates—down, up, and then down. For years, many of us subscribed to the theory that falling interest rates caused PE multiples to expand, and they were the driving force of any bull market. However, trends in the 1950s will convincingly demonstrate that a change in the direction of interest rates starts bulls, not a change to lower rates.

The executive summary is that we will experience the Reset in the next five years if we do not change our entitlements. Valuations of everything will decrease first with a "BANG!" followed by a long period of anemic economic growth. It will be the antithesis of the 1995-2000 boom and worse than 2007-2009 Financial Crisis. In the interim, you just have to play the rally and invest in stocks!

If we do get our house in order, stocks and real estate are the places to be. Avoid bonds at all costs.

PART V.
A THREAT TO DEMOCRACY

As a nation, our focus has not been on the key economic variables. Quite frankly, it has mostly been on everything else. And the political polarization of America is a product of unsound economic policies—it's not the other way around, as many people incorrectly assume.

While unprecedented amounts of monetary stimulus does have a steroid effect on the economy that is keeping us afloat, the longer fiscal policymakers continue to not "have their house in order," the higher the probability of the Great American Reset. The set of policies ushered in since 2009 as a result of the Crisis have promoted larger government and increased regulation, which decreases incentives and heightens uncertainty for business people to take risks and create jobs which will result in solid GDP growth. For democracy to survive, pro-growth economic policies and limits on entitlements are required.

How will these trends, left unaltered, affect our country? When will the other shoe drop? What can be done? What can you and I do?

CHAPTER 20
THE GROWING DIVERGENCES OF RED VS. BLUE STATES

Government view of the economy can be summed up in a few short phrases:
If it moves, tax it; if it keeps moving, regulate it; and if it stops moving, subsidize it.

~ Ronald Reagan

When we talk about economic theories, deficits, debt, taxes, and spending, these are applicable to many government entities—countries, states, metropolitan areas, and even smaller cities and counties.

Federal spending in the United States rose to over 25% of GDP in 2009, from just over 21% two years earlier. The stimulus spending allowed the bailouts of Fannie and Freddie, the $800 billion stimulus package, the mortgage relief program, the silly "cash for clunkers" deal, and the $600 per person tax rebate check.

And what did we get for it? Not a thing. Per the International Monetary Fund, member countries of the Organization for Economic Cooperation and Development (OECD), who spent the most on the stimulus, had lower economic growth rates. People know that this must be paid for with higher taxes. Typically, people who enjoy work do so a bit less when they are taxed more, and their displeasure is pronounced by the assumption that those additional tax dollars wind up in the hands of people who don't work.

This creates a difficult scenario for fathoming higher employment and economic growth. Stimulus spending at the country level just does not work.

What about at the state level? Do income tax rates of individual states affect one's behavior? Are there other driving factors?

The simple answer is yes it matters, and a better answer is jobs, jobs, and more jobs. These days, people are "voting with their feet" (moving to states with lower tax rates), and I'd expect this trend to continue, and become even more pronounced.

States where incentives and low tax rates are a part of the landscape are growing at the expense of the high and increasing tax-rate states. Art Laffer and the American Legislative Exchange Council promote limited government, free markets, and federalism. Their analysis revealed those states that follow their philosophies are more prosperous, in spite of federal anti-growth policies, compared to the struggling, higher tax rate, bigger-government states.

Incentives are important. The fastest growing metropolitan areas all have zero or very low tax rates. Businesses start their companies in these places—or relocate to them—which creates jobs and attracts people, economic activity, and tax revenue. Growth in state populations in the ten-year period of 2001 to 2010 were led by Florida, Texas, Arizona, Indiana, and Tennessee—all zero or low-rate states that are extremely well managed.

On the other hand, the list of how *not* to govern is long, led by California and their now 13% marginal tax rate. In the last ten-year census, they had negative population growth! New York, New Jersey, and Ohio likewise fall into this category of how not to manage, supporting high tax rates.

And what is each of these groups' commonality? The pro-growth southern states are primarily Republican Red and implement Reaganomics and the Laffer Curve. These tax-free states and their soon-to-be tax-free neighbors should create quite an economic oasis relative to their counterparts. The low-rate states are truly capitalist.

The northern states continue to get bluer, and not surprisingly, their tax rates continue to go up and environmental restrictions on oil and gas drilling remain present. They are highly unionized with state-specific higher minimum wage rules. "Fairness" is priority one, which makes economic growth anemic. The spiral continues. The poor get hurt the worst, just as Milton Friedman said in 1979 about all civilizations that he studied. These blue states are redistributionists. Laffer describes it as "doubling down on Obamanomics."

When we all eventually meet our Maker, many of us will pay Uncle Sam yet one more time—in estate and inheritance taxes. Forever a minuscule moneymaker for the federal and state governments, it robs families of their success and work ethic by taking approximately half of all their assets (after an exemption currently of the first $5 million) that they accumulated in their lifetime. Unbelievable. At the state level, many are incentivizing their residents to move to other low death-tax states, which is a very perverse economic policy.

Arguments from the blue states' viewpoint can be taken seriously or facetiously. Some blue states say they can't afford to offer red-like incentives, as their obligation of huge pensions, aging infrastructure, and unions restrict their ability to have lower taxes. Blues can't afford it. Well golly, Gomer! They are correct, and that's just the point! You have not taken care of yourself and now you want old red to pay—but red left for a more pro-growth world! "Sorry you ate so many donuts, Uncle Joe, but I ain't paying for your huge healthcare costs. I'm going to the gym!"

Golf Pro Phil Mickelson, a California resident, voiced his realization of the tax increase trend in early 2013. In January, he made 12% less after taxes than he did in 2012, as California tax rates went up 3%, federal tax rates went up 5%, and the Obamacare tax began at 4%—a total tax increase of 12%. When he balked that he should join Tiger in Florida, where tax rates are 0% (yes, 13% less than California!), the Professional Golf Association gave him grief. Some of my buddies said he should have kept quiet and just moved. I say bull! He should let everyone know why he voiced his consideration to move to Florida. Vote with your feet! This is a free country!

One more social issue should be mentioned regarding the growing divergences in Americans in general. The pro-business red states seem to have more traditional religious views and more children. Old relics, like *moi*, often say, "What a nice hard-working, fun-loving Christian family!" We desire limited government and low taxes—kind of self-sustaining.

The blue states seem to have a much higher percentage of "no religion" residents and a more European work ethic and style. Could there be an American vs. European or capitalism vs. socialism conflict on the horizon? How many people fear the mere acknowledgment of these theories? That's exactly what scares me, and exactly why I wrote this book.

CHAPTER 21
A GRAND BARGAIN, PLEASE!

The incentive that you give to your youth is going to be the make-or-break future of the country.

~ Abdallah II
King of Jordan

The "idealism" associated with the buildup of the Internet era was a feeling of overall optimism, yet caution. Something did not feel quite right, using everything I learned from my father, my schooling, and my nearly twenty years of investment experience.

It did not end well for most, as the 2000 crash, followed by 9/11, presented pause for everyone. As discussed earlier regarding the bursting of the Internet bubble era, I was both lucky and perceptive to "sell my baby" when the markets rolled over in 2000. We were in the bottom of the first inning of a long, painful decline.

As Michel Lewis wrote in the preface of the dot-com bust section of his book *Panic*, this cautionary feeling described as "idealism" seemed to have repeated itself in the presidential campaign of 2007. Today, a "change the world" mentality is visible all over America, just as it was in Silicon Valley in 1995-2000. I am forever fearful this desire cannot be fulfilled; note the charts in this book and the many inflection points in the last five to seven years. The world has indeed changed. Yet examining history as a sound means for glimpsing the future, it seems abundantly clear that the change is NOT going in the right direction.

America needs to be educated on the importance of sound economic philosophies, policies, and practices. Please spread the word. I would love for my children and grandchildren to live in an even better world than the wonderful one I have been so blessed to enjoy. A better journey should be in store, not a worse one.

VIEWS ON CAPITALISM

America's love affair with capitalism seems to be waning. In case you haven't noticed, I am worried sick and very upset about this! Raised upper-lower class and never afraid of a 70-hour workweek, I have seen, heard, felt, loved, and experienced the most remarkable life. And I attribute such fortune to capitalism. Sure, the Catholic foundation and being bestowed with an above median IQ has helped. But by golly, incentives matter!

Over a third of Americans do not view capitalism positively. I assume they think and hope that the government will create a job for them. Perhaps my naivety is being exposed by assuming that the majority even *want* a job, instead of preferring to live a subsidized, low-key, low-stress, slow-paced life. Yuck! I must be a dinosaur.

Over a third of Americans have been raised in a "no savings" environment, as many assume the government safety net will always be there. Alarmingly, the Pew Research Center for the People & The Press reports that 60% of the 18-29 year-old age group responds positively to the word "socialism." I interviewed six of my seven children who are aged 18 to 23 (not a typo—twins, twice!) and they all said they understand how socialism will never work. Yay! I am proud that my capitalistic mindset is not being tested with my children. As socialists always run out of other people's money, I am glad they want to make their own.

The inheritance tax is absurd. How do the masses get a higher quality of life? Jobs and opportunities are created by people willing to invest their capital. And I must apologize, but it is seldom the poor person who is creating a job for the masses. If you have saved money, there are only a few options as to what to do with it—consume it, invest it, or give it away. If you want complete consumption versus legitimate society-bettering investment, simply increase the estate tax to 100% and everyone will spend their money frivolously. By the way, the percentage of tax revenue the government gets from the death tax is less than 1%. This is yet another example of a silly economic policy. The ultra-rich liberals who want successful Americans to pay this tax have all set up their family foundations to pay fat salaries to their family… Can you hear me Warren (Buffet) and Bill (Gates)?

Why do we keep marching down the road to socialism when we all know it has failed, as has communism? Governmental endorsement to become a cab driver or a welder—is that what the American people really want? I doubt it.

No society has ever been advanced by nurturing the bottom—the antithesis of incentives. Such states reward the below-average, and subsidize the less fortunate at the expense of the ones who actually want to work 12 hours a day. The top must pull up the bottom through opportunities provided by those who are incentivized. The free-enterprise system works as a non-socialistic society by helping people help themselves.

In 2008, the liberals proudly proclaimed the collapse of Reaganomics. By 2012, even after getting a terrible report card, it seems the majority of our people are content to experiment with a European-style socialistic government. I don't think they know how to read the true stats on the scorecard, nor the score!

Small businesses are regarded more and more as the enemy in socialism, but that is where the jobs are created. If 50% of Americans pay no federal taxes, the welfare state is much easier to enter, and unemployment lasts a long time… Yet we focus on minuscule items such as cost-of-living-adjustments (COLA) for Social Security, countless hours on gun control, and other social issues—while Rome is burning!

In April 2013, the White House presented a budget with an economic message that was more of the same. Increased spending and higher tax rates from the private sector to grow an even larger government, extremely unrealistic GDP growth rates, more entitlement spending than ever (including billions for public works), high-speed rail, battery-operated cars, and other nonsense. I am amazed and have begun wondering what planet I am on. Still, days later, Professor Alan Blinder of Princeton, analyzed the proposed budget process, giving it "a pretty good grade." Another comic illustration of grade inflation which sadly missed the mark.

A CALL FOR LEADERSHIP

We need leadership! We are at a point in history where it's essential for our leaders to think beyond their personal preferences and goals. In order to lead this great nation, every policymaker should demonstratively show their genuine love for America—a signal that unquestionably boosts confidence and alleviates anxiety (remember the smiles of Reagan and Clinton, and the heartening presence of JFK?). I still get goose bumps every time I hear our *National Anthem*, and if you are in an elected position and you don't, I can't help but question your motives for pretending to lead. In fact, I fear that you just don't get what this country is all about!

We need our leaders to promote values that are losing traction in America. We need leaders who are willing to thank successful Americans for their creativity, drive, and determination—the ones highly likely to give back to this great country in oh-so-many fashions. Our leaders should understand what it meant for my great grandfather to travel from Germany without a nickel in his pocket to "the land of the free" and forge a life for himself and his family. He was successful because he loved to work! Our leaders should respect my father's dedication to the U.S. Navy and his minesweeping duties in Okinawa and Nagasaki.

In today's America, we see so much of everything but the above being rewarded by policymakers that I really believe our leaders forget that they are *elected* officials who are here to serve you and me!

CHAPTER 22
WHAT CAN WE DO?

The democracy will cease to exist when you take away from those who are willing to work and give to those who would not.

~ Thomas Jefferson

The best way to predict your future is to create it.

~ Abraham Lincoln

It seems we are in a new land, a transforming nation. Call it a revolution. The Crisis that started in 2007 presented an opportunity for the government to institute its worse than Keynesian-like fiscal policies, disguised as economic medicine. The slant and degree of one's political leanings—liberal, conservative, or otherwise—is eclipsed by the reality that this cannot go on much longer! Look at the European model of social democracy. Isn't it safe to say it's on a downhill slide? Yet we are adding a third healthcare entitlement program to complement the failed and already-bankrupt first two versions: Medicare and Medicaid. Pinch me—wake me up! In poker parlance, it's like doubling down on a pair of deuces when everyone knows Uncle Joe has four aces.

The U.S. keeps telling itself that we are different than everybody else. If we are, we won't be for long, staying on this unsustainable path of growing a mountain of debt. Soothsayers, such as Berkeley's Robert Reich, who profess loudly their disdain for responsible citizens who focus on the size of government and debt, are also wrong. They just don't get it! Their focus on poverty and equality is the perfect prescription for horrendous times for the common people. In good times, the world's tendency is to liberalize... to the point of a crisis. We really need to open up our eyes!

So what can we do? I recommend that each of us put our great country at the forefront of our minds, as change in the right direction will require each of us to do so. We must speak out loudly! I recommend the following items:

EDUCATE YOURSELF

I congratulate you and thank you for getting to Chapter 22. The purpose of this book is to describe in a non-technical fashion the current state of affairs in the United States, and clearly illustrate its unsustainable path. I hope I was successful in educating you in an enjoyable fashion.

Please do anything and everything possible to further your education about Team USA, and assist your loved ones in doing so. The best investment in the world is education!

But please don't stop here. Continue to educate yourself and spread the word. Yes, Congressmen and Senators—this definitely includes you. I'll gladly spend a day with any of you explaining the charts and concepts herein.

Rogoff and Reinhart's *This Time is Different* documented many types of financial crises in developed countries, and discovered they have a common element—an excessive amount of debt in good times without paying attention to the negative repercussions of WHEN, not if, the big recession occurs. The result is always a prolonged economic slump. Arguing otherwise simply denotes a lack of common sense. This may sound harsh, but unfortunately, there are many who lack such common sense. In severe economic crises, housing markets plummet for years, stock markets crash quickly, and unemployment worsens for years. Debt levels typically double. All in all, it's extremely painful!

Yet many still argue, "the U.S. is different" and/or "this time it's different." Well, my Mother would say, "Sorry Charlie." I was always schooled that if we ever break the buck on money market funds, the financial system was cracked. And we broke the buck. I also believed that Bernanke's tools from the 2002 speech would remain unwrapped in their original case. All the Fed additional tools are now in session.

It is a privilege to be an American—an opportunity to work hard and get ahead, educate yourself, help others, and more. Like every man, woman, family, and business in society, the USA has a financial responsibility! We keep conveniently forgetting that it is the foundation for all other rightful intentions. But we are failing miserably in that area. Professor Hafele is giving a D- grade, calculated by the sum average of an F for the raw grade, an F for the direction of the trends shown in the graphs, and a B for the consolation of being the greatest country on this planet.

READ ABOUT HISTORY and OUR CURRENT STATUS

Regarding our spending, our Founding Fathers would not only roll over in their graves, but they would stand up and shoot!

One is deemed to repeat the mistakes of the past, particularly if one remains ignorant to the occurrences. I'd like to recommend four books that could help us remedy our entitlement crisis, along with a brief reason why.

1. *The Bible* - The best-selling book of all time.

   No matter what religious persuasion you may have, the basic role of "love thy neighbor as thyself" remains at the forefront of liberty and equality in America. It says many neat things on how we have the obligation to take care of ourselves, too! Also, look at the Constitution and Declaration of Independence while you are in the mood.

The Catholic Church has voiced its disdain for socialism for nearly a hundred years. Why? It undermines the central truth of Christianity that man needs God. Socialism sets up man as god in construction of utopia (heaven on earth). Much has been written in the last five years about attempts to neutralize the Catholic Church by dividing it, similar to the way the leaders of the Prohibition movement divided the brewers and distillers to fulfill their anti-alcohol dreams. By the way, how'd that Prohibition idea work out? Uh, a regulatory, economic nightmare it was.

2. *Atlas Shrugged* by Ayn Rand

   The 1957 must-read describes a rather undesirable and frightening society, one collapsed by government intervention. Simply stated, the most productive people (the hero is John Galt) disappear from society. A Reagan favorite. *The Hunger Games* is a recent depiction of a dystopian society. A bit extreme but everyone should think entitlement societies through and recognize their terminal effects.

3. *Free to Choose* by Milton and Rose Friedman

   This 1980 magnificent piece illustrates the efforts of incentives and just how the free market works. Although I don't agree with their criticism of *all* central planning, understanding their train of thought is essential for anyone before they opine on our great country, including our chosen leaders.

4. *Rules for Radicals* by Saul Alinsky

   A prevalent theme of political activist and community organizer Saul Alinsky's book was that ethical rules need to be elastic to stretch with the times. Published in 1971—just a year before his death—the agnostic, Marx-loving man promoted rather unorthodox tactics. A condensed version called *Rules for Patriots* which summarizes the key absurd points in Alinsky's book has been circulated by conservatives in the last several years in an attempt to "know thine enemy."

SPREAD THE WORD

I hope that I have illuminated some areas in support of the big picture—entitlements are unsustainable! My objective was to explain the economic roller coaster of capitalism from a historical perspective and recognize that bumps in the road are part of life. But if you want capitalism to persist, the current trends must be altered.

Talk to your children and your siblings. Chat about this intelligently with your friends over dinner. Explain what is really going on—I'll bet you a liquid refreshment that most have no idea of the state of the union as presented in this factual book.

WORK HARD... and PROUDLY SO!

Many people, in various sections of the country or select demographics, prefer not to work hard. Or even work at all! As evidenced in the low labor participation rate, fewer and fewer people are working in today's America.

Now if you have saved for you and yours, and elect to live off the fruits of your labor— congrats! More power to you. But if you are just relying on the next government program to help you, shame on you. I am afraid that a rude awakening is just around the corner. I know that everyone is not healthy or educated or whatever. But do the best you can and work! America was founded as "the land of the free and the home of the brave," not the land of "How do I get things for free?"

Above all, be proud of your work! The opportunity for success and positive energy, generated from being self-supporting and successful are huge elements in living long and happy lives. If your spouse decides to work so you can purchase that new car or dream vacation, be super proud of it! You earned it!

If you collect Social Security in retirement, I congratulate you and wholeheartedly encourage you to enjoy the benefits. These were promised to augment your savings and assist you in your latter years.

BE RESPONSIBLE FOR YOU: SAVE and INVEST

And so, my fellow Americans, ask not what your country can do for you.
Ask what you can do for your country.

~ John F. Kennedy
35th U.S. President (1961-1963)
January 20, 1961 Inaugural Address

JFK, in his most famous line, was speaking of the need for all Americans to be active citizens and take care of themselves. By the way, JFK had a balanced-budget focus, and even signed a pledge to keep one.

Over the last fifty years, savings have gone the way of the Ford Edsel, 8-track tapes, and lead paint—virtually to extinction. And the reason why? You guessed it—entitlement thinking.

The Social Security Administration and the Bureau of Economic Analysis note that there is an extremely strong correlation between rising entitlement spending and falling personal savings rates.

Americans saved approximately 10% of their take-home pay until the 1980s, when people began taking on an increasing amount of debt that continued for 25 years. Entitlements were a low percentage of take-home pay—less than 5%—in 1970. They have now soared to approximately 25%.

Be responsible! Save for you and yours. Invest conservatively (but not too much so) and be wise.

CONTACT YOUR REPRESENTATIVE

Let your representative know how you feel. Few know or understand these apolitical economic facts. So many politicians live in a different and growingly untruthful world versus the free market economy.

Focus on the key variables of growth, unemployment, inflation, debt, and deficits. Ask the people to quit focusing on minutia—whether it be non-economic items we've discussed (environment, abortion, gay marriage, and whoever's "rights")—or making big deals out of nothing like the CPI (consumer price index) calculation for Social Security.

Sure, the Social Security tweak would be a move in the right direction, but in financial terms, it does not move the needle on our overall debt situation. Nor does it address the true problems directly associated with Social Security.

The recent bragging that the deficit is better, and that it was as low as 4% of GDP for this fiscal year, is absurd! Is that something to brag about? No, it is not. The tax revenue increase is a function of asset sales that occurred last year in anticipation of the capital gains tax rate increase. This revenue is a one-time occurrence, as it has been when rate changes occurred in the past, and subsequent years' projections are worse.

Please ask your representative to consider this basic and truthful approach:

1. Get educated and address the cold, hard facts—that we have structural, fundamental problems.

2. Ask them to do a little work that illustrates the causes of the problems and address those causes!

3. Do it now while it is still fixable. Wait another five to ten years and bye-bye capitalism. Establish solutions and act!

4. Stop the lies of all kinds, whether you deny challenges exist or act as if you are addressing the material items. We cannot afford to preserve the welfare state in its present form.

I would also like to challenge the print media to do their job, and resume reporting the facts honestly. Please get back to investigative journalism, and point out hypocritical political statements. Ask the hard questions, or otherwise you are headed for the trash heap along with yesterday's paper.

Our great nation is big business! It has to be properly piloted as we ride the American rollercoaster of capitalism. Incentives matter, entitlements have become corrupt. Business men and women propel our world, providing opportunities and jobs for the masses. There will be crises in capitalism, and the importance of sound economic policies will determine how severe and frequent the crises will be.

If we don't wake up, America, and change the trajectory of the charts in this book, the inevitable Great American Reset will materialize, and it will surprise many people worldwide. Let's reestablish our sense of pride in the USA—lest we share the fate of other fallen superpowers that litter the landscape of history.

PART VI. A HISTORY OF FINANCIAL CRISES

Much of what you have read in this book's first 22 chapters may lead one to believe that the Financial Crisis of 2007-2009 associated with the Great Recession was unprecedented. In some ways, that is oh-so-true. But in many others, there have been a number of crises that are eerily similar and predictable.

Financial crises have been around for centuries and come with the territory of booms and busts, inflicting much pain along the way. To alleviate the magnitude and frequency of the crises, the Federal Reserve was formed only to be soon followed by the Great Depression. Understanding this important period of history is paramount to understanding our current economic state.

Are there common elements in these financial crises? Absolutely yes. In addition to the crises, we will discuss some of the mini-crashes, each of which at the time seemed unbearable but were merely blips on the radar of American history.

CHAPTER 23
PRE 20TH CENTURY FOLLIES

As I've said before, these free money scams are a problem.

~ Matthew Lesko
American Author

Much has been written about human nature and our sheer madness. An objective analysis of economic policy will reveal that our religious preferences and political persuasions play very little role in restoring sanity to unhealthy financial systems. Throughout history, mankind has been delusional and the manifestation of madness among the masses is one of life's guarantees. To use a financial term, this has been proven again and again by the flourishing (and subsequent bursting) of bubbles. "Bubbles" occur when the valuation of something greatly exceeds its fundamental worth. Looking back in time, we can see that bubbles are also a part of life—except perhaps in communist economies, which by their own design have seen far fewer moments of euphoria than America has enjoyed in its young but magnificent life of innovation and ingenuity. Ours is a capitalist society, and if we want to enjoy those euphoric moments while riding the white-knuckled high peaks of the rollercoaster, we need to keep it that way.

Growing up in a large family was full of fun, laughter... and frequent disagreements. In the heat of the arguments, I was often scolded by my older siblings, who said, "Who does he think he is—Johnny Law?" Well, there actually was a real Johnny Law... and a bubble he did indeed create.

In 1717, Johnny Law formulated a plan to commercialize the Mississippi Valley to assist France's anemic economic state. He helped form the Mississippi Company as a director of the New Royal Bank, raising a speculative bubble for Louisiana land that was supposedly chock-full of gold and silver. This huge speculative bubble burst in 1720. Law's resume also included becoming a playboy in London and authoring numerous scams. He once dueled with and killed a rival, was charged with the murder, went to jail, and later escaped. He was the perfect example of an old-fashioned "flimflam man."

The "South Sea Bubble" in nearby England also failed miserably in 1720. Formed by Robert Harley in 1711, this scam persuaded owners of government bonds to exchange them for South Sea stock because they supposedly had a monopoly on trade between Britain and the South Seas. Well, the expectations of getting trade concessions from Spain never materialized, and the speculators lost their shirts!

Combined, the 1720 near-simultaneous collapses of the Mississippi Company in France and the South Sea Company in England brought into question the ability to create prosperity through credit expansion.

Nearly a hundred years earlier in the Netherlands, "Tulip Mania" became the first recorded speculative bubble, also known as a financial crisis. The term Tulip Mania is still used as a description when an asset is, for whatever reason, priced far above its true value. Tulips became a leading export at the height of their lofty valuations in 1637, when prices for one bulb exceeded the annual wage of a craftsman by nearly ten times. The mania spread from the wealth speculators to the middle class as a status symbol, a telltale sign that it was late in the game. The Dutch had developed the equivalent of today's futures market used by speculators and farmers. Trading on margins and illegal short-selling followed, resulting in a ten-fold run-up in prices in 1636, and culminating in a 90% crash.

These three examples clearly illustrate that mania issuing from panics and crises was not born yesterday. Hundreds of years have passed and, yes my friends, you and I are the insane distant relatives of these loonies, and quite prone to engage in the madness that creates bubbles and the ensuing financial crises. Charles MacKay, in his *Extraordinary Popular Delusions and the Madness of Crowds* is an excellent book on our craziness—written in 1841!

Financial crises occur due to the folly of human nature. They result in many business failures and include sharp asset value declines. Unfortunately, they cause major disruptions to our financial markets and, consequently, to our quality of life.

CHAPTER 24
THE FORMATION OF THE FEDERAL RESERVE

Our focus is on ensuring America has the strongest economy in the world for the next 100 years and to do that, we need to get the role of the Federal Reserve and we need to get it right.

~ Kevin Brady
U.S. Representative, Texas

Financial crises have imposed unpleasant realities on humanity for centuries. What does history proffer as a solution to minimize the frequency, as well as the magnitude, of such crises?

The answer lies in a brief history of the origins of the U.S. banking system. The first federal government-chartered bank—the Bank of the United States—was formed in 1791 as a combination of a private bank and a government-instituted central bank. It lasted just twenty years, as distrust among business people was prevalent and banking was preferred at the state level. A much larger central bank was reestablished in 1816 as the Second National Bank of the United States, but lasted only through its twenty-year charter until 1836. For over 25 years, there was no central bank. However, there was an abundance of problems with risky loans, insufficient reserves, and low levels of capital. Another attempt occurred when the National Banking Act of 1836 was formed without the ability to expand or contract currency in circulation, and resulted in booms and busts, panics, and depressions. Not having a central bank repeatedly resulted in large economic swings. Acute financial crises in 1837, 1857, 1873, and 1893 were all followed with depressions. Every twenty years or so, the reset button was effectively pushed, and there was plenty of pain and suffering.

Finally, in 1907, stocks crashed and there was a "run on the bank," that bank being the third-largest institution in the Knickerbocker Trust Company. Most of the people who had deposited their hard-earned dollars stood in line for many hours, withdrawing their savings because they had no faith in the banking system or the institution they had previously entrusted. With no central bank and no way to inject liquidity into the system, John D. Rockefeller stepped up, putting money into the markets to prevent a collapse. But he did not have enough assets to slow the downward spiral. J.P. Morgan, who did have enough assets, followed Rockefeller in supporting the markets. He created interest-bearing certificates to settle accounts between major banks, thereby freeing $80 million to inject liquidity into the banking system. Panic over.

But J.P. Morgan was 70 years old. The need for a central bank was evident. By 1913, the Federal Reserve Bank (known commonly as the *Fed*) was born. Safer banks for all! Financial crises no more!

The Fed worked diligently in its initial years during the 1910s, keeping rates low to finance World War I by increasing the money supply over 75%. Not surprisingly, inflation doubled by 1920. The Fed grew in its new Manhattan home in 1927, securing 10% of the world's gold. Few knew its first real test was looming just around the corner in the autumn of 1929, the topic of our next chapter.

Fast-forward to the 1960s, when Lyndon Johnson's "Great Society" resulted in deficit spending alongside the accommodating easy-money Fed led by Arthur Burns. Inflationary pressures increased. By the 1970s, we had created *stagflation*—a period of high inflat ion, low economic growth, and stubbornly high unemployment. The cause was excessive growth of the money supply, assisted by the oil supply shocks that drove gas prices up sharply.

With a checkered past by the early 1980s, the Fed finally stepped into the limelight of success with Paul Volcker at the helm. The "Misery Index"—unemployment and inflation combined—was running in the high teens. Volcker switched Fed tactics from the start-stop micromanagement of the money supply to a more steady growth rate policy. His effort to curtail the actions of his predecessors in favor of Milton "The Monetarist" Freidman's approach still goes down as one of the most successful economic policy changes in the history of our great country. Inflation expectations were successfully dampened, thereby triggering a 30-year plus decline in interest rates, a roaring stock market, and just an incredibly excellent era in which to live one's life.

Volcker's successor, Alan Greenspan, took the helm in 1987, steadfastly and stoically managing the money supply through 2006. He was considered the "Maestro" and was given an A+ grade by all—until the Great Recession cracks appeared in 2007.

Since its inception, the Fed's primary mandate has been to maintain price stability followed by maintaining employment at an acceptable level. With low-to-moderate inflation, the economy tends to grow moderately, jobs are plentiful, and crashes are rare. With the existence of the Fed, controlling the strings of capitalism seemed quite doable, and the common belief became that periods like the Great Depression would never occur again.

CHAPTER 25
THE CRASH OF 1929 AND THE GREAT DEPRESSION

The most striking development of the Great Depression of 1929 is a profound skepticism of the future of contemporary society among large sections of the American people.

~ C.L.R. James
Anti-Stalinist Journalist

The world was full of optimism in the Roaring Twenties, as so many people were materially increasing their standard of living. The Fed had been formed, thus drastically reducing the probability of recurring bank failures, if not eliminating them entirely.

Industrial production doubled in the decade. Stocks started a strong ascent in 1924. The American people displayed a huge appetite for getting rich; even more desirable by most was to get there quickly without a lot of effort. Florida real estate boomed as higher incomes and improved transportation that made it reasonable to "warm up" in the winters. Charles Ponzi (as in *Ponzi scheme*) earned his place in history as speculators bought subplots of Florida land. Stocks were bought on margin, and collateral requirements were lowered. The Fed strongly believed in easy monetary policy. Even land investments in the form of an option—the right to buy with a small down payment—were prevalent.

The good times prevailed, and few decision-makers wanted to puncture the party balloon. Calvin Coolidge was checking out, handing presidential powers to Herbert Hoover. The Secretary of the Treasury was Andrew Mellon, known by most as a free market guy who promoted the ideology that no change is best.

The Dow's ascent was changing the world, going up over 300% from 1924 through late 1929.

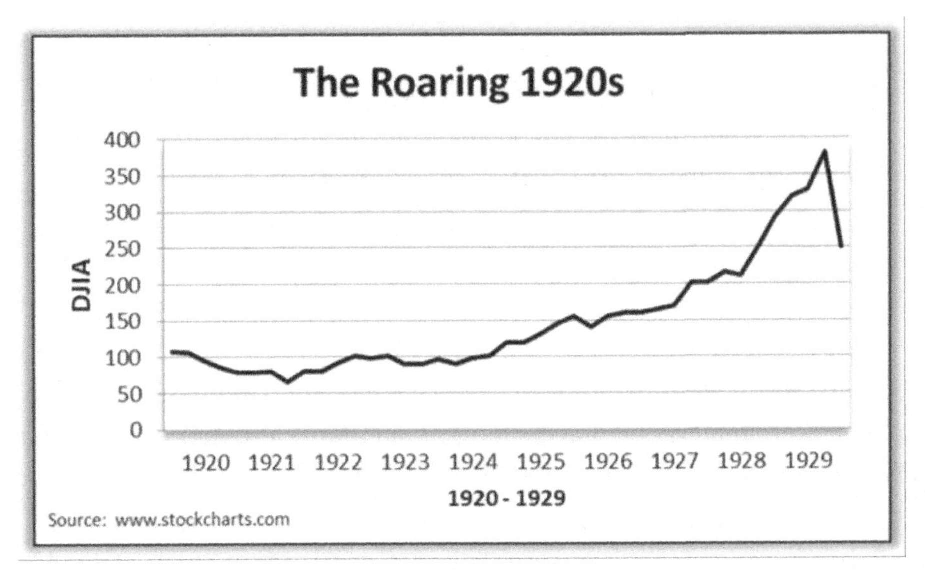

Such an ascent undoubtedly causes most all elements of economic growth to increase dramatically. Today we call it "the wealth effect," and that is exactly what it was in the 1920s. The stock market greatly influences the attitudes and risk appetites of those who have money, and—like it or not—they are the ones who create jobs, thereby influencing the overall quality of life for the masses.

An increase of this magnitude in the stock market greatly influences business leaders and investors. My friend always said a big bull market in stocks, à la the 1920s, is much better than his best tequila buzz. With speculators on every corner, and the supply of capital for everything growing, it was an excellent time to raise funds for anything while enjoying prosperity. The creation of investment trusts—investment vehicles that allow smaller investors to pool their assets together—allowed even more leverage, thereby proliferating dreams of getting rich quickly. Brokerage houses were crowded with average Joes, all watching the ticker tape and counting their money. There was continual assurance from the leaders of their day that "the fundamentals are sound."

As the market continued its six-year ascent into 1929, skepticism naturally was heard from some contrarian leaders. On September 5th, speaking at the annual National Business Conference, a well-known strategist named Roger Babson warned of an impending crash. Barron's and *The Wall Street Journal* both balked at his prognostication. But with the very next day came the first break with high volume. What followed was the beginning of the Great Crash that wiped out 90% of the Dow Jones Industrial Average over the next few years.

The 1929 Crash accelerated on October 24th (infamously coined "Black Thursday"). Many stocks had no buyers, thus creating quite a descent in price before an orderly transaction occurred. The nation's most powerful people all gathered to pool resources to support the market. Yet on Monday, October 28th, things went from bad to worse. Margin calls—when investors' assets fall below the required amount—were occurring daily. This forced additional selling, further propelling the downward spiral. The Rockefellers stepped in. The fundamentals of the economy turned south. The panic was so pronounced that the "organized support" was also selling—unfathomably adding to the carnage.

The markets finally bottomed in November 1929, but the descent reignited in 1930. There were large tax rate cuts by the Hoover Administration following the ideology of John Maynard Keynes but the additional dollars in the typical American's hands was so small and insignificant that the effect on the economy was virtually nil. Capitalism was very much in question.

President Hoover jawboned that everything would be fine. Banks suffered severely, and their leaders—somewhat shocked by the severity and reality of the sad economy—made unscrupulous bets and paid themselves handsomely. There was much finger-pointing between the government and Wall Street. Ugly times...

The effects of the 1929 Crash lasted for a decade. In summary, there was no progress in the 1930s, and painful it was.

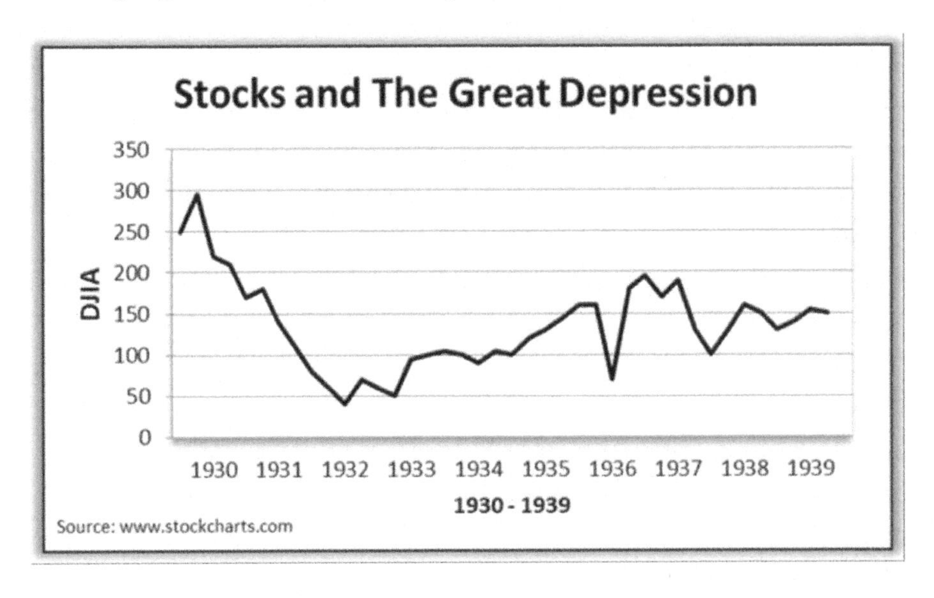

The Dow Jones Industrial Average plummeted in late 1929 through 1932, wiping out nearly 90% of the wealth people thought they had acquired. The Great Depression really lasted for the entire decade of the 1930s, as there were several rallies, followed by sharp corrections from 1935 to 1937. The volatility of the stock market further raised suspicion on the sustainability of capitalism and the free market system.

As a big fan of the consumer confidence surveys, I can only guess how low confidence was in this period, as the data was not collected. The leaders, the operators, and the government were all shocked and naturally contentious. Uncertainty was at its peak. Consumer confidence is a very important economic variable. It is the wise old sage of indicators that effectively summarizes all others, and its level and direction can provide a huge influence on the economy, markets, and overall quality of life.

The gross domestic product (GDP) went down over 25% in the 1929-1933 period, and it took until 1941 to get back to the June 1929 peak.

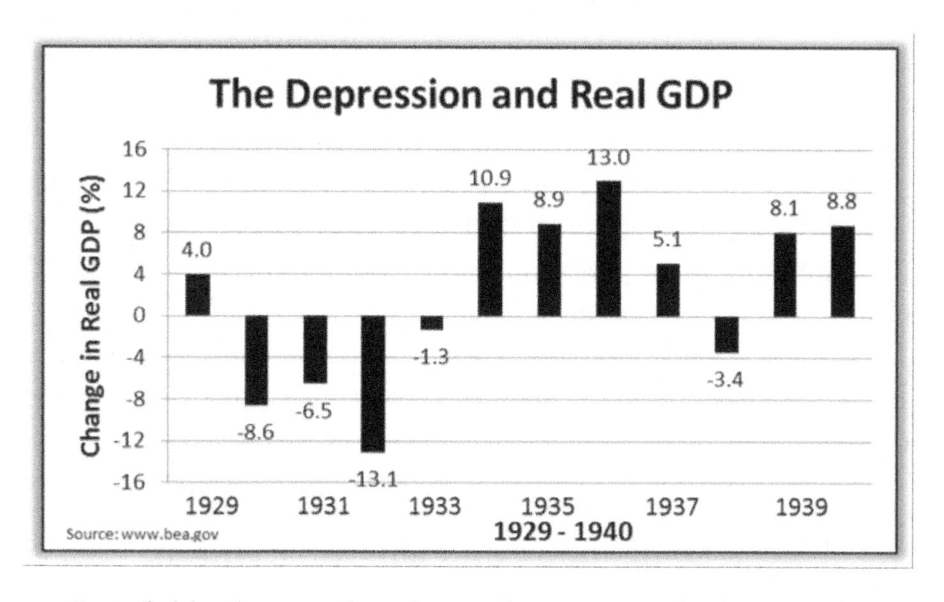

Periods like the 1930s have huge effects on everyday lives. Real GDP is the scorecard for the quality of our lives, and the beginning of the 1930s caused severe pain for Americans. An economic recovery developed in 1934 through 1936, but was then followed by a recession in 1937. The economy has always been cyclical in nature, but this period was cyclical on steroids! The cycle usually starts with much speculation followed by a period of prosperity. The economic cycle then usually peaks (as seen in 1929) and uncertainty heightens, accompanied by prophetic statements that all is well. In the early 1930s, confidence was crushed and the real GDP suffered dearly.

Whole libraries of scholarly material have been generated about the 1929 Crash and the subsequent Depression. Fed Chairman Ben Bernanke spent twenty years of his life studying the period. (I think I'd study something more exciting like the Roaring Twenties and the sins of the era.) The summary of these studies is that fundamentals matter! In the 1920s, productivity per worker was soaring, while wages remained rather stable. That greatly influenced the very highest income earners to create many jobs (naturally) and increase their personal net worth. In 1929, the top 5% earned 30% of the income, and the marginal propensity to consume for the rich was not very high. Corporate swindlers and fraudsters were everywhere with their holding companies and investment trusts. Individuals were terrified that their money in the bank was not safe, as banking laws lacked the safety net of the FDIC (Federal Deposit Insurance Corporation). And the domino effect of any bad deal on any bank was significant.

The stock market decline triggered the economic slump of the 1930s. Even more dramatic than the anemic GDP growth rate was the unemployment level.

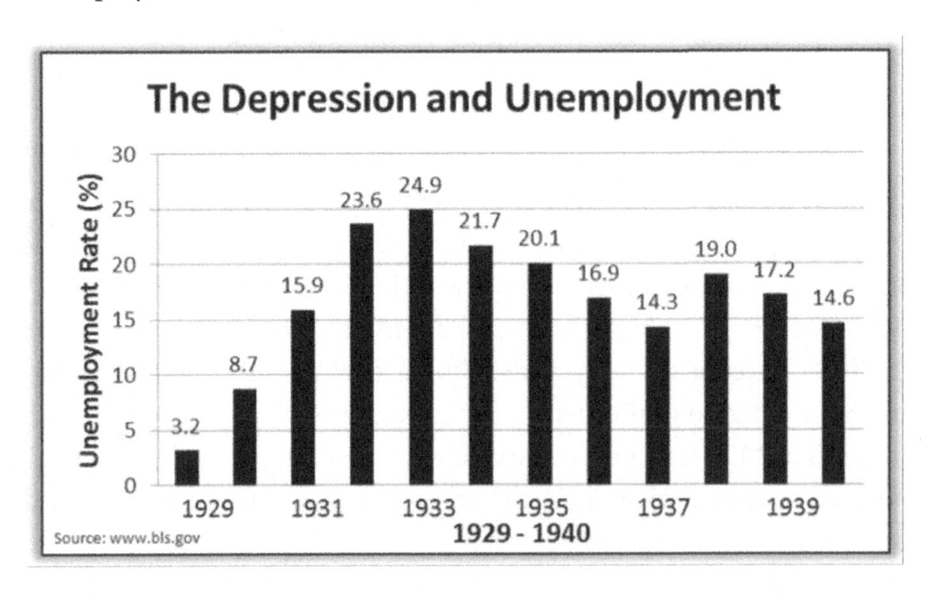

After the crash, the unemployment rate soared to nearly 25% by 1933, and remained above 14% for over a decade.

So why was this financial crisis so enduring and so pronounced? The answer—throughout history and the subject of this entire book—is improper economic policies.

First, the Fed, still virtually in grade school and less than 20 years of age, didn't react well and effectively "put it in reverse." They increased interest rates prior to the crash in a fruitless attempt to prick the bubble. In October 1929, they reduced the money supply, thereby moving the economy into a slowdown. From 1929 to 1933, the amount of the money supply decreased about the same as the GDP contraction of 25%. Deflation figures were over 25%.

It is safe to say that the monetarist school of economic thought had not yet been born. Economists did not understand that the velocity of money—the number of times a dollar gets spent—typically falls sharply in recessionary periods and even more so in a depression.

In addition to the monetary policy faux pas, the fiscal side came running in 1930 with reckless abandonment. Categorized today as an increase in regulation and an effective tax rate increase, the infamous Smoot-Hawley tariffs were enacted, which included a 50% increase in tariffs on all imports. Volume shrank 50% as Hoover ignored economists' pleas to veto it. And yes, tariff revenue plummeted from the higher tariff rates. Jobs were scarce and nowhere to be found.

President Hoover then more than doubled tax rates in 1931 and President Franklin D. Roosevelt raised them again in 1936 (to 79%), thus reducing incentives significantly for anyone to invest or create a job. The economic spiraling-down continued.

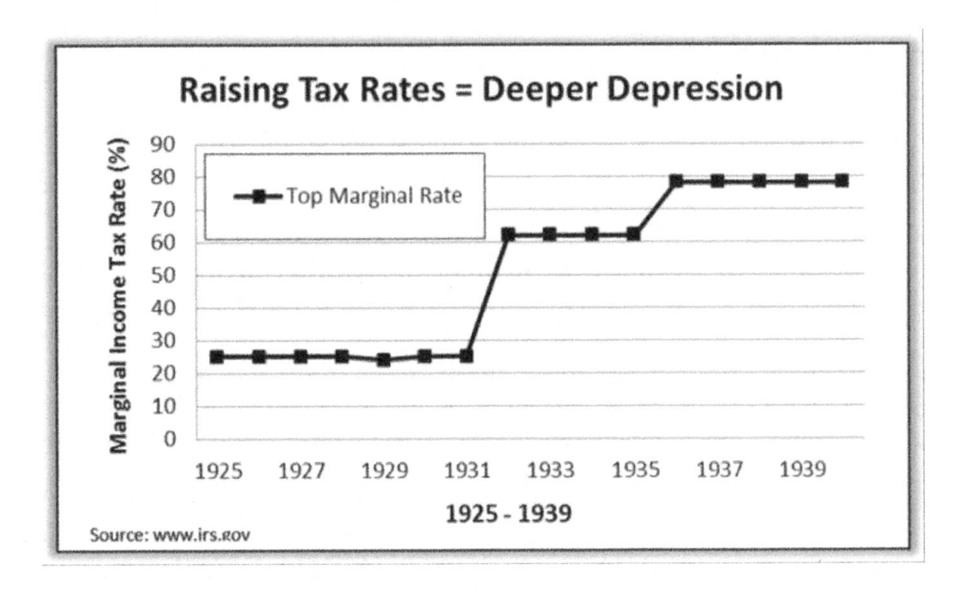

This is an excellent example of slowing economic progress by raising marginal tax rates! Additional taxes on those who invest and create jobs—the people who tug at the strings of capitalism—results in higher unemployment.

With uncertainty levels higher than ever before, the economic policy moves—most of which were in the wrong direction—bred even more uncertainty. The onset of FDIC insurance—where the government would back up any failed banks—lessened depositors' anxiety and reduced the probability of a "run on the bank." Perhaps the New Deal was a good policy move, but it has never been proven (it could have been responsible for the prolonged contraction as discussed in Chapter 10). Attempts to influence the "invisible hand" that controls prices and supply-and-demand relationships were fruitless. The creation of rules regarding quotas, wages, hours worked, etcetera applied to most everyone, and resulted in a caging of the animal spirits. If there was ever an era that the country needed to unleash those animal spirits of incentivizing, it was then. The market process was completely undermined! An F grade for President Hoover.

The Great Depression was triggered by the Great Crash of 1929 and it fueled incorrect and ill-timed economic policies. The duration of horrendous economic times was extensive, saved only by the subsequent focus on defending capitalism during World War II.

The effects of economics and the importance of the craft were now evident. As this book stresses, the study of the economy throughout history is very important because it greatly affects our standard of living. In the Depression, both fiscal and monetary policies were backwards. Knowledge of the multiplier effect was in its infancy. Tariffs were added, further thwarting economic activity. The Depression ensued. Deficits were around 2% of GDP, and in the worst years of 1934 and 1936, they were approximately 4%. A comparison to today's even larger deficits has been discussed earlier.

In conclusion, much has been learned from the unfortunate circumstances arising from 1929. Personally, I benefitted greatly from my "priest uncles" guiding my father and, later, me in life. So much for never meeting my true grandfather. But for the majority of us, the realization that economic policies have a huge impact on our everyday lives became evident. That's why all of us should hasten to increase our "Economics IQ" by studying history and policy effects.

In addition, the effect of the "Great Crash of 1929" on the businessperson and the wealthy was pronounced. And, like it or not, I have never seen many jobs created by poor people. We must have sound policies that incent the more fortunate to grow GDP at a sound and solid rate. This creates jobs for America.

Lastly, ethics is paramount. Much of the blame of the Depression can be assigned to the unscrupulous and then POW! A blowup ensues and we all pay the piper. We have to regulate, but we have to be extremely careful with the amount of regulation, always focusing on stimulating the animal spirits. Regulating society is a dangerous game, as unintended consequences are an inevitable byproduct.

CHAPTER 26
COMMON ELEMENTS IN FINANCIAL CRISES

More people would learn from their mistakes if they weren't so busy denying they made them.

~ Anonymous

Financial crises from every era throughout history share certain common elements. Omnipresent is the existence of asymmetric information—which is simply where one party knows more than the other. Economists divide asymmetric risk into two buckets with their own labels: (1) "adverse selection" if one party knows more than the other before the transaction, or (2) "moral hazard" if one party engages in undesirable behavior after the transaction. All business people seek to minimize asymmetric risk in any fashion, but there are times when these efforts fail. To minimize adverse selection, banks require collateral, people rely on rating agencies, and investors trust that audited financial statements are indeed correct. To reduce moral hazard, people prefer to deal with owners and principals who have personal funds involved rather than managers; this is known as the "principal-agent problem." Conflicts of interest are part of capitalism. All of these potential conflicts are seeds that may grow into real problems. If they grow quickly and become large, economic activity contracts, volatility surges, and a financial crisis is born.

For years, I have utilized in my finance classes a textbook written by former Fed governor, Dr. Frederic Mishkin, simply titled *Money, Banking and Financial Markets*. He does a fabulous job of describing why financial crises occur, the factors that cause them, and how crises typically play out. Many of the ideas and explanations in this chapter emanate from my studies of Mishkin's way of thinking.

The initiation of a financial crisis can be started by a host of factors. A large increase in uncertainty—either from a stock market crash or the start of a recession—generally gets the crisis brewing. Typically, asset prices—whether stocks or real estate—are driven up higher than normal. Alan Greenspan's "irrational exuberance" comments in 1996 regarding stock prices provide an excellent example. A bubble is born and it eventually does what all bubbles eventually do—they burst. New laws or products deemed as financial liberation or innovation are part of the landscape and are either managed improperly or they produce unintended side effects. Another factor could be a quick rise in interest rates, resulting in lower GDP growth.

Yet another factor in financial crises is a significant deterioration of the balance sheets of financial institutions. As loan losses grow in the early stage, capital requirement amounts enter the picture and banks start the deleveraging process, providing virtually no loans and thus an economy without enough liquidity. In the deleveraging process, individuals simply decrease the amount of debt for which they are responsible—whether it is debt on their house or their business.

The initial stage of a financial crisis can also be caused by fiscal imbalances of government. Washington—please take note! As soon as creditors catch a whiff of the fear that a government may default on its debt, a crisis materializes. The prices of bonds fall and the health of financial institutions' balance sheets further deteriorates. Such fears can create a crisis for a country's currency, resulting in a foreign exchange crisis as investors pull their money out of the country.

Whether it is asset declines, uncertainty spikes, bank deteriorations, financial innovation, a rise in interest rates, or government fiscal imbalances, a crisis brings out the charlatans! Asymmetric information problems worsen. People who have the capacity to borrow—creating economic activity and jobs—fear risking their futures in order to borrow. People that perhaps should not be borrowing—already levered up with weak balance sheets—get the bank door slammed in their face. The initial stage of the financial crisis then worsens.

The second stage of a financial crisis involves a banking crisis. As businesses contract, national levels of uncertainty rise again, even to the point that investors withdraw their funds from the banks. What happened in Cyprus in 2013 is a perfect example of the second stage. Typically, panic ensues. Banks are declared insolvent or at a minimum issued a "cease and desist" order by the Fed, effectively neutralizing them from making loans and profits.

The proverbial "run on the bank" was a part of all financial crises until World War II. They occurred every twenty years in the 1800s and again in 1907. And everybody who had any money left in 1929 stood in line to withdraw it as the Great Depression gained steam.

Through the bankruptcy process, investors are then sorted out as solvent or not solvent (incapable of paying their debts). Banks experience the same process with the help of regulators. The cleansing occurs and the seeds are sown for a reversal and a new start to the whole cycle. The stock market recovers, interest rates fall and, eventually, uncertainty fades and positive economic activity returns.

But occasionally the financial crisis is more severe, and we unfortunately experience yet another stage before any recovery materializes. Debt deflation is the third and final stage, characterized by a sharp decline in prices. In the U.S., the Great Depression provides the ultimate example of how severe all the economic figures may look if step three materializes. The recovery process is short-circuited, as hits to net worth and increased debt burdens overwhelm stimulating policies. Adverse selection and moral hazard are so prevalent that progress is halted—to a standstill. The most recent financial crisis, dubbed the Great Recession, indeed experienced stage three as the stock market declined 50% and housing prices declined 30%—a previously unimaginable combination in modern times.

Much has been written about the current status and trends of the United States' fiscal imprudence. Financial crises do indeed develop from fiscal imbalances, and those effectively looking the other way ignoring the inevitability of a crisis are simply wrong! (We have discussed history and these key levels in prior chapters.)

What about financial crises of emerging market countries? Yes, the progression of their crises is very similar, but with a few differences. The initiation stage for countries in their early development phase either experience huge fiscal imbalances or mismanagement of the financial liberation process. Fiscal imbalances—and thus debts—need to be financed. Eventually, no investor or bank will buy the credit as all attempt to unload the existing owned paper, causing further deterioration. Business people whose personal interests outweigh the taxpayers' often pervert the financial innovation process. Sometimes, weak banking supervision results in huge loan losses, accelerating the downward spiral. Package unstable political systems with smaller stock markets and less collateral, and one easily can see why crises may occur more frequently and be more severe in smaller countries.

The second stage for emerging markets is much more detrimental than the USA's second stage banking crisis. In emerging markets, a currency crisis develops as the factors in stage one grow upon each other. Speculators bet on the depreciation of the currency and the government has no power to defend itself, as raising rates needed to attract capital thwarts economic growth.

As the currency depreciates, the country's debt burden increases into stage three—a full-fledged financial crisis where the downward spiral continues for a long, often torturous, period of time.

CHAPTER 27
RECENT MINI CRASHES: 1987, 1997, AND 2000

Financial crises are like fireworks: they illuminate the sky even as they go pop.

~ Anonymous

In less than a 20-year period, there were three mini-crises before the Great Recession in 2007. The first—the 1987 stock market crash—was the beginning of a new period of crises. These financial blips affected our lives in many ways, albeit for just a short while in hindsight. Next, the Asian currency crisis and the Russian government bond default in 1997 further suggested something new and unusual was in our midst, giving pause and raising concern about the simplicity of our financial markets. Finally, in 2000, the bursting of the Internet bubble was heard around the world.

THE 1987 STOCK MARKET CRASH

The Dow Jones industrial average fell 22% on October 19th, 1987. *Twenty-two* percent… in one day! Opening at 2,247, by the four o'clock bell we had dropped 508 points ending at 1,739. Personally, it was a day of infamy—one I'll never forget.

As an eager young portfolio manager just 29 years old, there was not a thing to do that miserable day but stare dumbfounded and amazed at the Quotron machine. Were we experiencing reality or just daydreaming a nightmare? Volume was multiple times the norm, and all the records were shattered—a phenomenon that persisted for weeks. The systems were not functioning well at all, and any thoughts of diving into the mêlée did not seem prudent. Buy or sell? What will the clients say? We watched. Numerous clients phoned in with human social concerns. They were not worried about their assets, but instead spoke supportively; one even implored us not to jump from our 23rd floor window. Tough day. "Program trading" had overwhelmed the system and soon thereafter became a household word.

Portfolio insurance drove the 1987 Crash. It is simply the equivalent of an insurance policy on a portfolio of stocks, accomplished by hedging it against the overall market. By selling short stock index futures, the value of the portfolio will be steady as these investment vehicles (called "futures") go up in value while the market goes down. If the market declined further, theory states, one should simply short more market futures, thereby further protecting one's assets.

How did this "portfolio insurance" concept come to fruition? It was a combination of four developments—the Black-Scholes option pricing model, portfolio insurance, increased computer power, and index arbitrage.

The Black-Scholes option pricing model was created in 1973 by Fisher Black, Myron Scholes, and Robert Merton. (Poor Bob—left out of the namesake and deprived of branding his own name.) This invention led to a real boom in option trading and the rapid growth of the Chicago Board of Options Exchange. The model calculates the price of a call or put option with a rather complex formula that includes many assumptions. Having studied the model ad nauseam during my graduate work in the early 1980s, Black-Scholes was extremely useful, primarily for larger corporations and investors, to calculate the value of any outstanding options in a speedy fashion.

Building on the option pricing model, Mark Rubinstein from UC Berkeley invented portfolio insurance in 1976. As computer power on our desktops grew rapidly during the next decade, more and more pension and hedge fund managers were protecting downside risk of their portfolios by selling short the S&P 500 (Standard & Poor's) index as it fell, theoretically avoiding any down swoon in the market.

In addition, another trading strategy called "index arbitrage" was gaining momentum. This strategy exploits value differences between the futures contract on the market index and the index itself.

The market was ripe for a crisis in late 1987, having advanced 28% in 1985, 23% in 1986, and 44% in 1987—just weeks prior to the crash. The total increase of 125% in two and three quarters of a year was eye-opening! Valuations were over 20 times earnings versus longer-term averages of 14 to 16 times. The Fed was methodically raising rates, influencing price-earnings multiples to contract, which results in a market decline. My instincts that "something different" was about to occur were correct. I also encountered a great contrarian indicator in this period: my extremely bullish boss.

During the prior months, the market had corrected just over 10%, triggering more and more managers to purchase put options as portfolio insurance and downside protection. When the market tried to open on October 19th, 1987, orders were so out of balance that the opening was delayed. Selling was highly concentrated with the "portfolio insurance" managers.

Importantly, the Fed briskly came to the rescue on October 20th, flooding the system with liquidity, and thus improving market conditions. In short, the market recovered nicely from the stock market crash of October 1987. By the end of the year, the Dow Jones Industrial Average (DJIA) finished 1987 in positive territory—up 2%. And the immediate years following were more than quite good ones, also—up 12% in 1988 and 27% in 1989. The world experienced yet another recovery from a would-be severe crisis.

The official causes of the 1987 stock crash, per a report by Mark Carlson of the Federal Reserve, were margin calls, program trading, and the difficulty of getting reliable information. “Margin” is the stock market’s word for debt and leverage, whereby assets are pledged for a portion of investment. If the value of the investment declines substantially, more assets are needed—and a “margin call” results. Many investors received margin calls at the end of Thursday, October 19th. Banks extended credit and managers further levered their bets.

Portfolio insurance contributed greatly to the crash, although it is still argued by some that other regular sources of selling were equally at fault.

Reliable information regarding prices contributed to the mayhem, and many elected to “run with the herd.” Here, the madness of the crowd and the delusions appear yet again.

One forever vivid memory in my lifetime occurred after the close on that fateful day of October 19th, 1987. Manual D. Mayerson, a client of my employer Sena & Weller in Cincinnati, was a wonderful gentleman and brilliant entrepreneur. A real estate tycoon, “Manny” phoned around 4:30 p.m. to chat about what just happened. With distrust for public markets that had grown immensely over the last eight hours, he requested a 7:00 p.m. meeting in his office just two blocks away. Mr. Mayerson requested that we price out his portfolio and bring it to the meeting—quantifying the lashings of that day.

Upon arrival, with sweat flowing from my shins (never before, never since) through my grey suit pants, Manny inquired if I drank bourbon. At the time I did not; I’ve since matured into a bourbon connoisseur, especially during the winter months. A long pause ensued. Before I could respond, Mr. Mayerson answered his own question, “Well, I don’t either but we both are going to tonight!” Oh my! The balloon of tension deflated instantly. The meeting was amicable and professional. He elected to hang in for a while as the market recovered, then retreated from the big bull in favor of a 6% plus municipal bond portfolio.

Only a crisis can create such a memory.

1997 SOUTHEAST ASIA and RUSSIAN COLLAPSE

Financial market liberation took another victim in Southeast Asia in 1997. The noteworthy effect of this crisis is that it took ten years to get incomes back to 1997 levels.

Crony capitalism was ever-present in Southeast Asia. Having maintained high interest rates to successfully attract foreign capital, assets inflated and GDP grew 8% plus throughout the late 1980s and early 1990s. Southeast Asia was described as an Asian economic miracle.

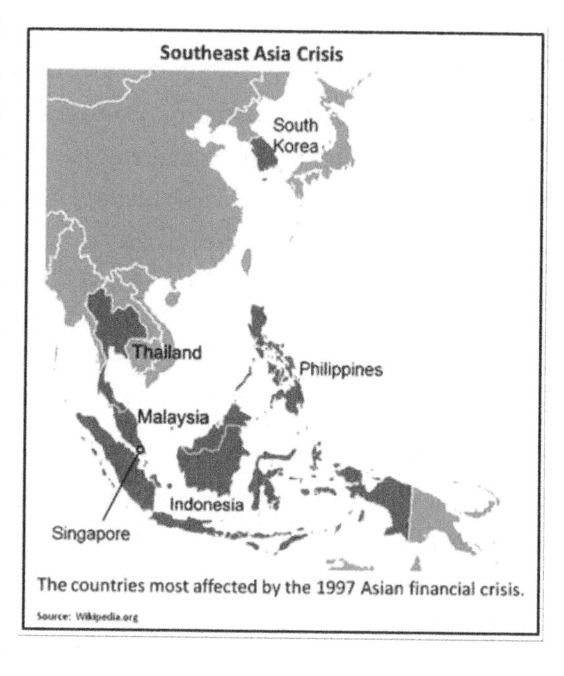

The countries most affected by the 1997 Asian financial crisis.
Source: Wikipedia.org

Then a severe overextension in the real estate market in Thailand culminated in the commencement of the Asian Financial Crisis of 1997. A formidable deterioration in banks' balance sheets occurred as a result of mounting loan losses. The Thai baht collapsed due to a lack of foreign currency to support its fixed exchange rate, which was tied to the dollar. The government was forced to float the value of the baht. Prior to the collapse, Thailand had acquired so much foreign debt that it put them into bankruptcy.

The crisis was most widespread in Indonesia and South Korea and to a lesser extent Malaysia and the Philippines. The Association of Southeast Nations countries represented nearly 10% of the world population, and they increased their combined debt as percentage of GDP from 100% to 167% in the four years of 1993-1996. The crisis was indeed a punishment for its sins.

The International Monetary Fund (IMF) assisted with a $40 billion program to stabilize the countries, but with mixed results. Several recessions ensued, as did the old-fashioned "run on the banks."

The contagion spread to Russia in 1998, as its ruble fell and so did the Russian stock market. Prices plummeted on Russia's two valuable resources: energy and metals. Chaos ensued as GDP fell, unemployment soared, and investors ran for the exit doors with Russian assets. Coal miners went on strike regarding unpaid wages. Investor confidence went through the cellar. The World Bank and the IMF stepped up with a large loan, and $5 billion was stolen on arrival just hours before the meltdown. Inflation increased to over 80% in 1998. In August, Russia defaulted on its Treasury Bills, devalued their ruble, and declared a moratorium on all foreign payments.

Yet another remarkable recovery followed from the seemingly severe crisis. A rise in oil prices in 1999 followed, and the devalued ruble and associated expensive imports drove a rapid recovery in the domestic industries.

In the 1990s, many emerging market countries opened their markets to foreign capital, only to experience severe financial crises in a somewhat predictable fashion.

2000 BURSTING OF THE INTERNET BUBBLE

Everyone recalls the early days of the Internet. Getting our email address from AOL and having the kids tie up the phone lines was fun! The long Internet buzz sound ending with a convincing connection beep. 1995 was the start of a truly spectacular era!

The environment everywhere was called "exuberant" by many. A combination of the "wealth effect" from high growth rates, very low unemployment, controlled and very moderate inflation, and controlled fiscal budgets had all of us very, very optimistic about the future. And times really were good! Since 1982, notwithstanding a short setback in 1990 with the Gulf War, the USA was on a roll! So with 13 years of momentum, forever increasing 401(k) balances and solid annual bonuses, by 1995, consumer confidence was off the charts. Times were excellent! And then, our generation's once-in-a-lifetime changing innovation came along in the form of the Internet.

The DJIA ascent summed up the pre-game party.

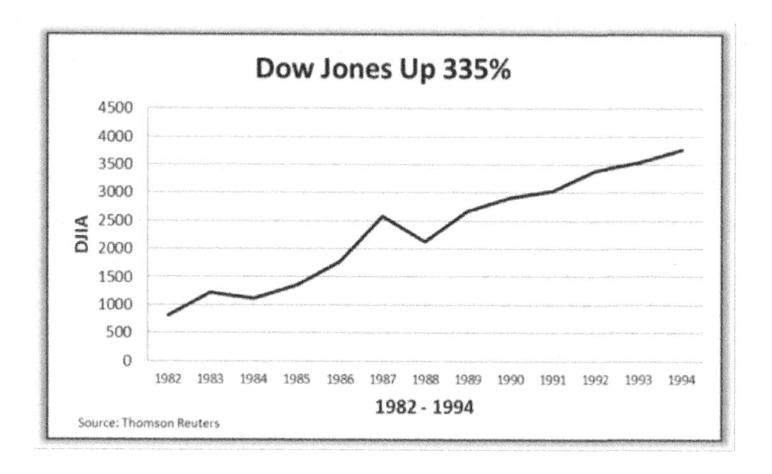

The market delivered an annual rate of return of 15% per year from 1982 through 1994.

So how about a nightcap?

OK, let's! What grew to be forever known as the dot-com bubble was now in its infancy. Driven by technology, the overall economy began skyrocketing in 1995. Venture capital money was available to all anywhere, and traditional metrics for valuing companies were associated with yesteryear.

The NASDAQ index, with the vast majority of its stocks being in the technology sector, soared at a meteoric rate.

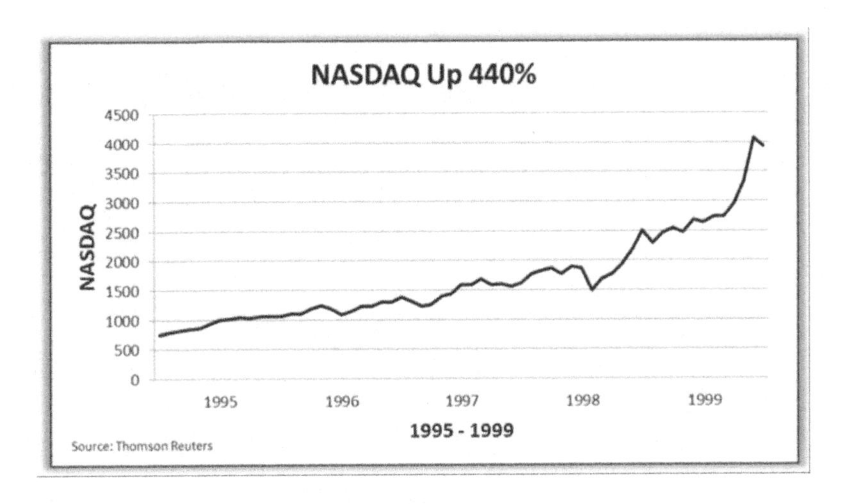

The annual rate of return was over 40% for the five years from 1995 to 1999. And the overall market partied hard as well, delivering very nice returns, propelled by the technology sector. The annual rate of return for the DJIA was extremely healthy—over 25%—in the same five years.

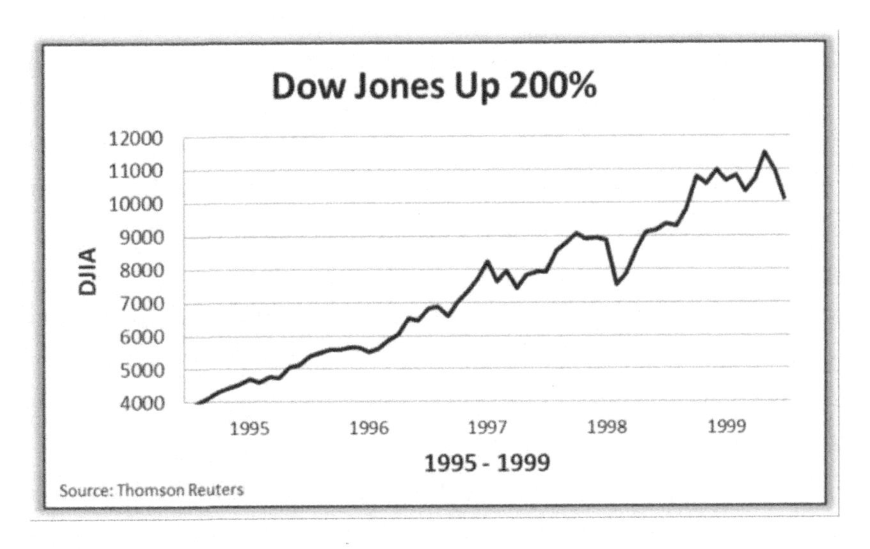

Combining the 1982-1994 era with the 1995-1999 period, one truly obtains a picture of beauty.

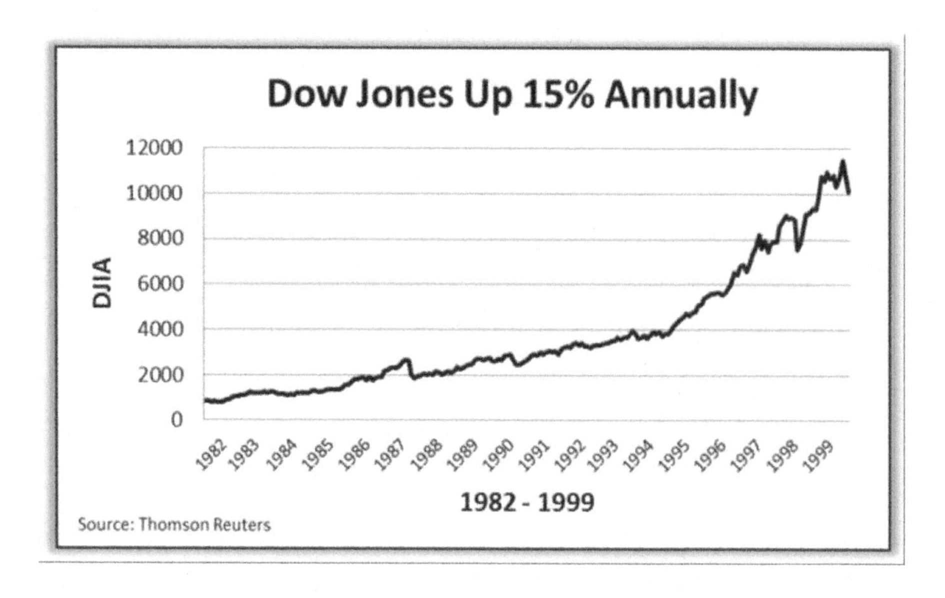

The annual rate of return on the DJIA was over 15% during the 1982-2000 market advance. The Dow went from 875 to 11,497—cumulatively an increase of over 1,200%. So investors that invested solely in the stock market increased their net worth twelvefold! Total return including dividends was 18% per year. What a run for nearly twenty years! Recall that in average or "normal" times, stocks deliver total returns of 10-11% annually.

Why is the 2000 stock market mini crash so important to economic history? The answer here is just like the analysis of the other financial crises— they are preceded with incredible periods of prosperity. "Happy Days are Here Again" is the best musical description. I would bet anyone long odds that the baby boomers will unfortunately not get to experience this once-in-a-lifetime period of prosperity again. I hope I am very wrong, but history suggests not.

In 1995, the initial public offering (IPO) market went crazy. Futuristic companies went public without ever delivering or even promising to deliver a profit! In hindsight, that sounds extremely silly. With promises of synergies, B2B (business-to-business), Internet speed growth, and more, fuel was put on the fire by unscrupulous Wall Street analysts-turned-investment bankers. They recommended companies to simply obtain underwriting fees. A modern day gold rush was at hand.

But it all started to unfold in early 2000. Companies were running out of cash, and caution was in the air as there were few if any sources of cash available. Wall Street strategists and their bullish sentiments had run their course. Washington profoundly emphasized that their focus was on the economy and everything was sound. Not a lot of difference versus Hoover's 1929 comments. Super Bowl ads featured companies who spent half of their capital in 30 seconds as they strived to become a household brand.

The NASDAQ plummeted.

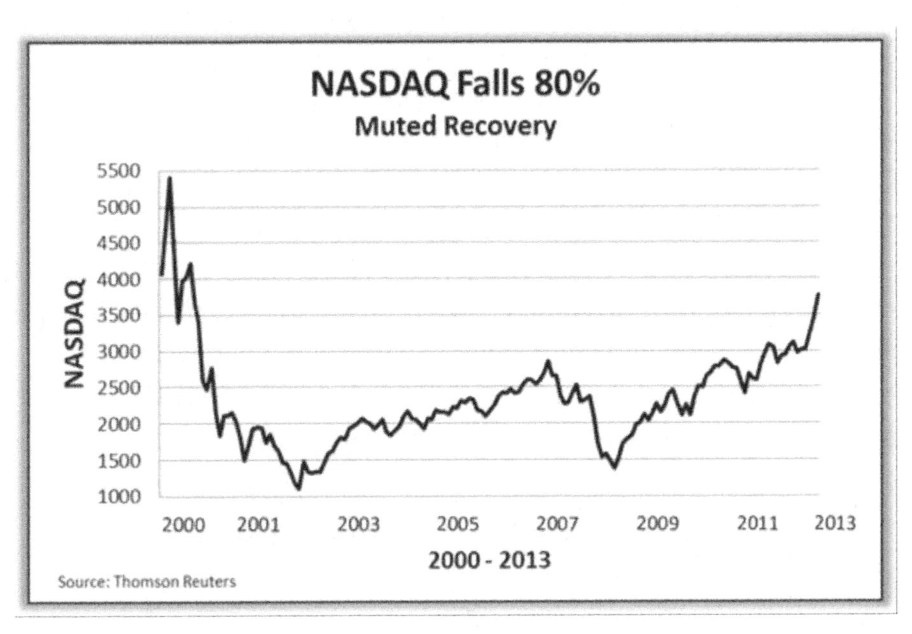

From its peak of 5,409 on March 10th, 2000, the NASDAQ fell all the way to 1,108 in October 2002, down 80%. Its recovery was rather tepid, rising up to just 2,812 in November 2007 before the Great Recession. There has been a little more strength in recent years, but it is still some 30% below the peak of 13 years ago. What a crazy dot-com bubble!

Yet the overall market recovered rather methodically and quite convincingly.

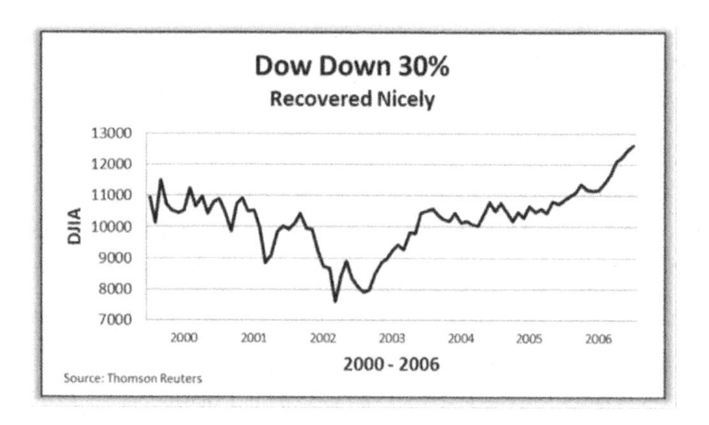

From the highs of 11,500 in 2000, the DJIA fell 30%—a pretty formidable bear market, but nothing like the technology bust of the NASDAQ.

A recession ensued in 2001, fueled by the large stock market correction, which was an overdue calming of the euphoria that commenced in 1995. The recession was then exacerbated by the terrorist attacks on September 11, 2001.

But the incredible resilience of Team USA showed up again! Pundits predicted tough times to come led by a decrease in consumer confidence and the negative wealth effect from a 30% stock market decline.

Greenspan sped his way to the rescue, dropping the Fed funds rate to under 2% in 2002—a level previously unimaginable.

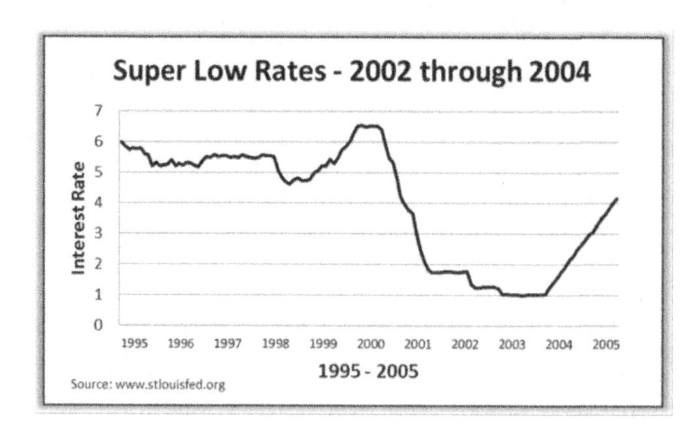

And the Fed kept rates low until 2004, when it commenced a series of 16 one-quarter to one-half percent (¼% to ½%) increases in a row.

The stock market crisis of 2000 had the common elements of euphoria on the front side, fear and panic in the middle, and an orderly recovery at the end.

MINI CRISES: A SUMMARY

Financial crises have been around a long time and are an unfortunate part of capitalism. Some argue that they are fortunate, as each crisis corrects the excesses to subsequently allow more efficient and faster growth. They occur on a somewhat regular basis, and the existence of the Fed is essential to attempt to lessen both the frequency and magnitude of the downturn. They each have common elements, yet have a few major contributors unique to themselves.

Complexities of the markets of innovation have increased the probability of crises. They seem like Armageddon, but economies recover with great resiliency—but only with solid economic policies! Large or small, it can be amusing yet painful to relive the moments. The amusing part is that the solution seems quite obvious… once the catastrophe has ended. The painful part is reliving your actions (or lack thereof) and reactions to the blunt reality of yet another financial crisis.

Michael Lewis wrote *Panic* in 2009, which I highly recommend. It has a host of various articles of the day in an attempt to understand these mini crashes. Every crisis has a "feeling in the air" buildup before the proverbial poop hits the fan, followed by attempts to deal with the disaster.

I hope and pray that the Inevitable Great American Reset does NOT materialize. For our hopes and prayers to be answered, much of the current way of thinking must change—and change soon! God bless America!

Made in the USA
Columbia, SC
22 March 2022

58004254R00124